The E-Business Workplace

Workplace

Discovering the Power of Enterprise Portals

John Wiley & Sons, Inc.

New York • Chichester • Weinheim • Brisbane • Singapore • Toronto

This book is printed on acid-free paper. ∞

Copyright © 2001 by PricewaterhouseCoopers LLP and SAP AG. All rights reserved.

Published by John Wiley & Sons, Inc.

Published simultaneously in Canada.

SAP and mySAP.com are trademarks of SAP Aktiengesellschaft, Systems, Applications and Products in Data Processing, Neurottstrasse 16, 69190 Walldorf, Germany. The publisher gratefully acknowledges SAP's kind permission to use its trademark in this publication. SAP AG is not the publisher of this book and is not responsible for it under any aspect of press law.

This publication is designed to provide accurate and authoritative information in regard to the subject matter covered. It is sold with the understanding that the publisher is not engaged in rendering legal, accounting, or other professional services. If legal advice or other expert assistance is required, the services of a competent professional person should be sought.

Library of Congress Cataloging-in-Publication Data:

ISBN 0-471-41830-7

Printed in the United States of America.

10 9 8 7 6 5 4 3 2 1

Contents

Foreword

The computer has transformed our lives. Business, being a part of life, has felt the full brunt of the ongoing technology revolution. What began as a tool whose potential was to automate tedious, repetitive tasks has grown to be the underlying force of a new economy that has swept away traditional notions that have defined business for more than a century. Bricks and mortar companies are taking advantage of e-business opportunities. Supply chains and cooperation have given way to value chains and collaboration as companies form value networks and compete within virtual marketplaces. What of the individual? Where does he or she fit within the broad and ever-changing e-business panorama? For individuals, has the computer fulfilled its promise of increasing productivity, enriching the work environment, and increasing job satisfaction, or has it become the feared and fearsome agent of relentless and sometimes incomprehensible change?

As information technology executives, we have long been concerned about one indisputable consequence of advancing technology: As computer technology grows in sophistication, it more and more defines the way people work, forcing working individuals constantly to reengineer established processes. The result? Increased stress and higher costs. As we have carefully monitored this phenomenon at our company, we have often wondered why software designers could not create products that were flexible enough to work *with* rather than *against* people, their processes, and their roles within a business. The problem only becomes more acute as e-business evolves into the dominant business model of the twenty-first century.

In some ways, information technology, while part of the problem, has supplied some of the solutions. Enterprise resource planning (ERP) software has helped to integrate data and streamline processes within individual companies. A plethora of e-business software products has promised to speed up and smooth out communication among business partners. But despite such promises, no technology has emerged that would dramatically improve intra- and inter-enterprise efficiency and effectiveness and reduce the growing need among employees to acquire more and more skills required to work effectively with increasingly complex applications. Not, that is, until now.

The hottest development in the Information Systems (IS) world is the emergence of workplace technology. The components of this technology—a host of "enterprise portal" software products—are currently in various stages of development by the world's major software companies. Their goal? To provide a new and powerful technology that enables the creation of a personalized workplace on the computer of each and every working individual who uses one. For the first time, this technology, with its richness of applications and its role-based design, makes possible the standardization of business practices among all of an organization's employees, suppliers, and business partners, regardless of geographical location.

In general, technophobes find it difficult to use and benefit from an ERP system run in the traditional mainframe or client-server model. With workplace technology, however, even casual users can access complex systems through Web browsers on their computer screens. Using ERP software can be, essentially, as easy as using an Internet-based consumer portal such as Yahoo!. Data from such systems can be combined with information from many other sources—including other companies along the value chain and third-party research services—to help improve the personal performance of working individuals throughout the company.

Moreover, each workplace is tailored to a specific job or "role," providing users with access to precisely the tools they need to perform their jobs most effectively and efficiently. Workplaces are also customizable, enabling working individuals to add components geared to their specific interests and needs. In short, this is a revolutionary technology that executives and managers in any company and any industry cannot afford to ignore.

This book serves as a comprehensive introduction to the concepts that drive workplace technology. The author team is made up of PricewaterhouseCoopers and SAP® consultants who worked closely together to write it. These consultants have been instrumental in the design of the mySAP Workplace—one of the leading new workplace technologies—and have had years of experience installing SAP's products.

The authors clearly explain—in language accessible to all corporate leaders and managers, not just to information technology professionals—how workplace technology can transform an organization by empowering its employees and those of its value network partners. Equally as important, they discuss in detail the competitive advantage that workplace technology confers upon organizations willing to embrace it. Along the way, they answer such questions as:

- How does workplace technology help a company to move from integration to true collaboration?
- Is workplace technology people friendly?
- Is there a convincing value proposition for workplace technology?
- How does workplace technology help people fulfill their roles within an organization?
- What are the "nuts and bolts" of workplace technology software?
- Can workplace technology increase business value and help an organization manage change?
- Where does workplace technology fit within the broader e-business context?

In answering these questions, the authors provide numerous down-to-earth scenarios and examples that give the theory behind workplace technology a real-world practicality. They also provide an indispensable discussion of lessons learned, based on the thousands of technology implementations in which they and their organizations have been involved.

At Nestlé, our commitment to workplace technology is clear. In June of 2000, on behalf of our company, we finalized an arrangement with SAP to place the mySAP Workplace on more than 100,000 computers used by Nestlé people worldwide. In addition, once the software is installed, it will also be available to our major customers and suppliers for their transactions with Nestlé. We fully expect to reap the tremendous benefits of this technology as we position Nestlé for future success.

To executives at organizations considering a similar commitment, or even to those who just want to get educated about this profoundly important technology, we cannot recommend this book too strongly. To them we say, read it, learn from it, and profit from its recommendations. Doing so just might make the difference between success and failure in an increasingly complex e-business environment.

Jeri Dunn	Jean Claude Dispaux
Vice President and	Senior Vice President
Chief Information Officer,	Group Information Systems
Nestlé USA Inc.	and Logistics, Nestlé

Acknowledgments

Writing this book has been a team effort. We are particularly indebted to the extended group of individuals who helped us with this project. Their contribution has improved our work and lightened our burden. We would like to take this opportunity to thank them for their dedication and invaluable assistance.

The author team would like particularly to acknowledge co-authors Dave Duray and Matthias Vering, who initiated this project and whose vision, guidance, and leadership were instrumental in seeing it through to its completion. We thank them for an opportunity to learn, share, and develop ideas with some great new friends.

We are also very grateful to those of our colleagues who generously agreed to review early drafts of our manuscript: Ric C. Andersen, Kay Baumgartel, Ed Berryman, Jeanette Bourke, Fred Byron, Michael Campbell, Mark Finnern, Volker Flottau, Mark Friend, Felix Giebfried, Anthony Gladden, Brian Glover, Peter Graf, Marty Homlish, Larry Hupka, Klaus Kreplin, John Leffler, Martin Moser, Shannon E. Myers, Hasso Plattner, Richard Ramsden, Adrian Samuels, Deborah Schmidt, Mike Schroeck, Jeffrey Schwartz, Elke Speliopoulos, Guenther Tolkmit, and Peggy Vaughan. Their insight, advice, and fresh ideas sharpened our thinking and improved our manuscript. We particularly appreciate the many hours of personal time they devoted to this project and extend our sincere thanks for their dedication.

In addition, we would like to acknowledge the other individuals whose contributions helped to make this book possible. In particular:

- Joel Kurtzman for ongoing advice and counsel. Your encouragement and expertise made a huge difference.

- Tig Gilliam and Lori Steele for helping us with current ideas and information on e-markets and for providing constructive examples. We appreciate your help.
- Peter Bundschuh, Stefanie Desch, Michael Obergefell, Beth Russell, Kurt Schwechheimer, Stefan Troska, Rainer Vetter, and Marcus Wandernoth for their extensive work producing and testing the CD-ROM included with this book. Thank you for your dedication to making this important component of our message a reality.
- Nelia Brito, Maureen Connolly, Anne Goertz, Kathleen Meyers, Joy Thras, and Dawn Wellbelove for administering this project, for organizing and coordinating our meetings over three continents, and for copying and distributing countless versions of the manuscript. We thank you for your patience with our impossible deadlines and for all your excellent work.
- Andrew Alpern, Frank Doll, and Edward Silver for providing us with legal advice and constructive feedback. Thank you for guiding us through a complex arrangement.
- Mike Smith for reviewing and updating our graphics, which are such an important part of the book. Thank you for sharing your gift for detail and accuracy.
- Bernhard Hochlehnert for providing us with great insight into the publishing process in Germany. Thank you for your invaluable support.
- Sheck Cho and members of his editorial and design team at John Wiley & Sons for helping us in ways too numerous to mention. Thank you for working tirelessly on our behalf.

Finally, we would like to thank our families for their unflagging support during the many months it has taken us to complete this project. Truly, without their understanding and support, this book could not have been written.

The Author Team

Introduction

Thousands of years ago, people began to produce goods for reasons other than personal use. Those who were skilled at making spears traded them with others who were good at weaving fishing nets. Those who were skilled at building plows traded them for food with others who used the plows to farm.

Over time, trade became a more formalized, structured process, evolving from one-to-one transactions into many-to-many exchanges. Those who made plows, spears, and fishing nets traded them all to a single individual at a central location, receiving other goods they needed in exchange. Farmers brought food to a trader, who, in exchange for their food, supplied them with other goods —spears, plows, and fishing nets, for example. On a many-to-many basis, trade proved to be both more efficient (i.e., less work) and more effective (i.e., a greater range of goods were available to all.)

These trading partners produced goods in their own workplaces, usually their own homes. Individual artisans creating products for trade—and later for sale—formed the basis of manufacturing until the industrial revolution. Each artisan's workplace was individualized; a weaver's workplace was different from a blacksmith's, which, in turn, was different from a boat builder's. Yet there were similarities among all of these workplaces. All artisans needed a place to store materials, tools, and records about their purchases of materials and their sales of products. As commerce became more complex, producers of various goods to buy, sell, and trade gathered in marketplaces throughout Europe and Asia, and later the Americas and Australia. Marketplaces made the complex trading process more efficient and effective.

Over the past 200 years, business has become increasingly large and complex. During the industrial age, less skilled generalists used machines to produce goods that formerly required the skills of specialist-workers. Ironically, these generalists soon became

1

the new specialists—operating one particular machine in a manufacturing process. Since the middle of the twentieth century, with
the introduction of computer technology into the manufacturing
process, the pace at which goods could be produced accelerated
dramatically. Computer software technology, with its linear logic,
drove production into ever-more rigid processes, forcing individuals—specialists and generalists alike—to conform their activities
and tasks to specifically "engineered" processes.

Today, at the dawn of the twenty-first century, commerce is
undergoing another radical change. Workers are seeking to dis-
aggregate themselves from many of the rigid processes of the corporate world. They wish to work for companies whose businesses
have been broken apart into smaller, more flexible, and personalized units. Those who continue to work for larger corporations are
asking for more flexibility in their working environment. Many
are seeking the option of working from home, or setting up small
offices as company satellites hundreds or even thousands of miles
away to avoid having to relocate to take new and better jobs. Customers are also demanding that employees of their products and
services suppliers be able to work from customer sites and that
sales and service personnel become hubs of communication between customer and supplier.

Today, the technology required to transform such scenarios
into reality already exists. Internet-based technology, integrated
with sophisticated corporate databases, knowledge management
methodologies, and decision support systems, makes possible the
creation of computer-based workplaces and marketplaces that are
the digital equivalents of the artisan's workshop and the town's
market square.

WORKPLACES

A workplace is a personalized front end through which an individual can access all the information, applications, and services
needed to perform work. Such computer-based workplaces use
Web-based interfaces to provide employees with access to all the
information, applications, and services necessary to perform the
tasks they must accomplish on any given day. The worker need not
know the source of the information, its format, or how, techni-

cally, it is pushed to the desktop. The underlying structure is completely transparent, and access is via the Web browser.

Workplace = Enterprise Portal

Workplace is a word not often used in a computer systems context. Portals is the more common term, specifically those portals developed by single companies for the benefit of their employees and external partners. These are often referred to as enterprise portals.

The portal concept originated in the business-to-consumer (B2C) world as a jumping off point for shopping excursions on the Web. Freeing consumers from the burden of finding specific Web sites on their own, a portal provides a starting point, a home page that appears on the consumer's computer screen when he or she logs on to the Web. A portal can be thought of as the on-ramp to the information highway, or as an opening to a large system of caves. From the portal an individual can go in many directions and from within any chamber, go to a deeper level or into one of many sub-chambers.

The portal itself provides clues as to how an individual can traverse the Web, either through navigational hints, such as menus, tabs, and hierarchies, or through information retrieval methods. Most portal home pages can be customized. For instance, most provide an area that displays current stock market information. Individuals can tailor this area to display only those stocks they are tracking. Typically, consumer-oriented portals provide access to news and weather reports, lottery numbers, and favorite Web sites. Some offer Web-based e-mail services, access to software downloads, comparison pricing of popular products and services, search capabilities, sports scores, music sites, and more.

Enterprise portals are the business-to-business (B2B) equivalent of the consumer-oriented portals after which they are modeled. But rather than offering access to consumer goods, services, and information, enterprise portals are designed to give each individual using them—executives, employees, suppliers, customers, third-party service providers—a unique view of the company providing the portal. An individual's home page in the portal is an analog to the workplace for the artisan of old—hence our use of the term workplace to describe the most sophisticated enterprise

portals. Within this virtual workplace individuals can find all of the
business information, applications, and services needed to perform their jobs:

- Information consists of consolidated data from inside the
  company's internal systems, as well as information from
  outside sources such as industry associations, the trade
  press, and information-focused marketplaces.
- Applications consist of job-specific software tools.
- Services consist of job-related assistance provided from inside or outside the company.

As they would with an office, a cubicle, or even a mobile work
station, individuals can customize this virtual workplace to organize information, applications, and services in a way that is most
comfortable to them, and to include some specific information
that they may desire. The specific information, applications, and
services to which any particular individual may have access is determined by the system's internal logic, which is driven by the
roles any particular individual fills. A person's role is not synony-
mous with his or her position in the corporate hierarchy. In fact,
an individual usually fulfills more than one role within an organization. These roles provide the framework for the activities and
tasks the person undertakes as part of the business processes that
assure the accomplishment of corporate goals.

Although essentially the same as enterprise portals, workplaces
exhibit a level of business intelligence. On the workplace, roles define the information, applications, and services available to any
particular person.

Information, Applications, and Services

The workplace focuses on delivering information, applications,
and services that support the company's core business processes.
Information might include research reports, economic data, and
trade magazines and journals. Applications include the full range
of software the company uses to conduct business. The workplace
can also serve as a gateway to the acquisition of services (as distin-
guished from the production of physical goods). These might be

available from both internal and external sources and could include such services as payroll, benefits management, and billing.

Information and applications available on the workplace are often embedded in services. For example, an employee whose tasks include the overnight shipping of packages would have access to FedEx, which provides not only pick-up and delivery of packages, but also information about where the package is, package volume shipped weekly or monthly, and even volume to individual customers or business partners. Using the FedEx software, the service purchaser prints a FedEx label complete with bar coding information and the information about the transaction is sent directly to the FedEx database for future tracking and transaction summary generation. When purchasers of FedEx services have Web access to both the processing application and relevant information about their packages, they feel in control and secure. Providing such information over the Web is also more efficient for FedEx, which otherwise would have to employ service representatives to respond to customer inquiries.

If the responsibilities of that same employee included making travel reservations, his or her workplace would also include access to Web-based travel services that provide a wealth of information about prices, travel times, and routes. The travel management service can actually process tickets, deliver them (or confirm for e-ticketing) and provide travel summary information for individuals, groups, offices, or even entire companies.

The Workplace Front End

Employees access the workplace using single sign-on to open a Web browser (Figure I.1). With single sign-on, an individual need only log on once to the workplace system to access all of the underlying systems, such as the company's ERP system, a third-party application, or an information Web site. Prior to workplace technology, users had to sign on to each system separately. The workplace provides individuals with true e-business potential, allowing them to tap into all of the technology and information tools necessary for e-business to occur—customer relationship management (CRM), supply chain management (SCM), e-commerce, business intelligence, and other back-office applications; Web services, and

Figure I.1   The Workplace

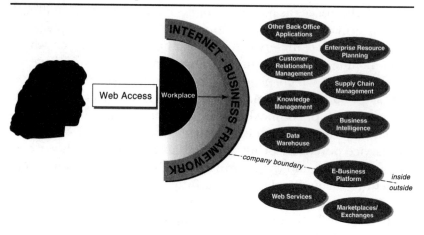

enterprise resource planning (ERP), data warehouse, and knowledge management systems.

The workplace is not limited to the PC. With the growing use
of mobile Web devices, individuals can take their workplaces on
the road anytime, anywhere. The workplace provides secure access
from any location. According to the workplace concept, all a user
needs is a Web browser and Internet access; no additional client
software is necessary. Once a user has logged on, he or she has secure access to Web-based tools that provide fast movement of data;
e-business tools that create consistent, reliable, timely, and accurate information; and enterprise application and information integration tools, commonly called middleware, that link software
components from many different manufacturers so that they can
work together.

Industry-Specific, Role-Based, Personalized

The workplace is industry-specific, role-based, and personalized.
Employees use the workplace in a way that is personally comfortable, taking advantage of as many or as few as they wish of the available navigational tools to bring appropriate content to bear on
their day-to-day activities.

What we mean by *industry-specific* is fairly obvious: information, applications, and services accessible through the workplace are relevant to an appropriate industry. For example, a purchasing manager for a chemical company would not have access to Web-based trading exchanges for the auto industry, but only for those within the chemical industry. The electronic library would include such journals as *Chemical Week*, not *Machine Shop News*. The workplace, therefore, reduces the amount of irrelevant information available to any individual by pushing, or making available, only the data most relevant to a particular role.

What we mean by role-based and personalized, however, requires a bit more clarification. Each individual in an organization fulfills one or more roles. In order for an individual to fulfill a role, he or she must undertake specific activities and tasks. A role is not a job. For instance, an individual can fulfill the roles of employee, member of a project team, relationship manager with a particular business partner and so on, all at the same time. The logic embedded in the workplace allows an individual access to only the information, applications, and services necessary to fulfill his or her particular role or roles, not the full range of information, applications, and services available on the system. This is what we mean by *role-based*. For example, a sales manager's workplace would include CRM applications but would not include those that support SCM. However, the sales manager would be able to reach the supply-chain applications for information purposes if he or she needed them. For instance, a customer might call and ask the sales rep about the status of an order. In this case, the sales person could access the SCM application for information gathering purposes, but because of his or her role, not have access to SCM applications that actually manage the supply chain.

By *personalized,* we mean that individuals are able to produce from information, applications, and services customized packages of presentations and content that they need and want, in ways that make them feel most comfortable. For example, one company's chief financial officer (CFO) may want to see his or her company's stock price and competitor's stock prices on the first screen, while another's might want his or her first screen to display company projects that are in the financing stage. Additionally, individuals may change their workplaces to personalize information and to facilitate current work habits and new tasks or activities that are added to their roles. The issue is one of control. The company controls the material available to the role, while the individual controls the personalization of that material.

An additional feature of the workplace is ease of navigation, for instance through "drag and relate" capabilities. Drag and relate refers to a seamless integration of different systems that individuals can view and utilize. For example, when presented with an order, a sales manager might want to check the customer's record. On the workplace, he or she could drag the sales order—called a business object—to the "display customer" function and relate it to the customer's entire sales history with the company. He or she could do the same with courier information, dragging data about a package generated by FedEx desktop software directly to the customer's company Web site. Relevant information from the courier about the shipment would appear on the workplace. Because of the collaborative nature of workplaces and the ability of the technology to handle changes simply and dynamically, the cost of implementing changes to current internal business processes can be reduced.

DERIVING VALUE FROM THE WORKPLACE

The lure of new technology stems from the potential benefits it promises to deliver. However, before committing significant amounts to the purchase of new technologies, a company must carefully weigh its ability to derive actual value from the investment.

Before committing to any investment, decision makers should rigorously analyze the potential benefits, quantify those that are tangible, and try to extrapolate a quantifiable benefit for those that are intangible. The workplace, however, offers a new set of tools that can provide much benefit—tangible and intangible— to many companies and their employees.

Companies Are Building Workplaces

In 1999, GartnerGroup wrote that enterprise portals "are one of the hottest new Internet technologies," and predicted that by mid 2002 "the number of viable horizontal Internet portals will decline while the number of vertical Internet portals will more than double." Workplaces will greatly assist large, global companies in taking advantage of this trend.

The Workplace Is the On Ramp to the Marketplace

Marketplaces are becoming increasingly critical components of the e-business economy. Marketplaces are business hubs on the Internet through which companies can buy, sell, or trade goods, services, and information with current business partners or with new customers or suppliers. Through the workplace, employees can enter a world of marketplaces, either those internal to the company or those open to all parties.

A marketplace provides a meeting place for an enterprise and other businesses and professionals to perform collaborative forecasting, conduct commerce, match requests for proposals and requests for qualifications (RFPs and RFQs), and interact in professional trading communities. As business hubs, marketplaces can serve as clearing houses for the exchange of documents and as business directories. Through marketplaces, workplace users and other community members can access industry-specific products, services, and content such as industry reports from analysts; information about trends and events; general content, such as news, sports, weather, and stocks; and chat rooms or hosted forums related to their roles.

Workplace technology can greatly assist companies in gaining access to relevant marketplaces. Collaboration will be the key to success in the new economy. Those who have their workplaces up and running at the right time and for the right reasons will be able to provide the platform upon which collaboration with business partners will take place and will position themselves as leaders within value networks. Those that do not may be left behind.

Individuals Are Key to Corporate Success

While the big picture advantages are clear, the workplace also brings additional benefits that are "closer to home." The workplace concept is driven by an overarching principle: Each individual is responsible for a company's success. Providing each individual with the right tools is the key to employee satisfaction, customer satisfaction, and, ultimately, shareholder value. Helping people to use information to do a better job is a valuable contribution to their satisfaction, as it signals a message that *they*, not the information systems, are the key to success. Companies that embrace the workplace concept view individuals as providers of corporate value, not as costs incurred and resources used.

The workplace benefits both the company and employee. Employees are empowered through a workplace that gives them access from any location to the information, applications, and services they need to do their jobs. A company utilizing a workplace strategy can improve employee productivity while opening up the possibilities for telecommuting, job sharing, and a host of other employee opportunities. The workplace's ease of use and focus on the individual's role helps break down resistance to change and creates support for improved business processes. Finally, the workplace allows the company to add new information, applications, and services, while reducing the cost and time necessary to obtain, implement, and manage them inside the company. In short, workplaces are the next step in e-business.

In this book, we examine the ramifications of workplaces for businesses of all kinds and provide insight into how most effectively to exploit their full potential to companies seeking success in the present and future e-business environment. We also include a CD-ROM that features the mySAP Workplace—one of several leading enterprise portal products—to provide readers with a hands-on demonstration of the tremendous potential of workplace technology.

1

From Integration to Collaboration

Very quickly Internet technology has forced companies to change the main thrust of their business system architectures and organizational dynamics. Whereas enterprise integration was once considered the key to success, savvy companies are presently striving to achieve extended-enterprise cooperation. And, as Web-based technologies continue to proliferate and take hold, links between members of an extended enterprise will become even tighter, requiring business models based on collaboration rather than cooperation.

The movement from integration to cooperation to collaboration is reflected in the evolution of the various empowering technologies that successful companies have embraced. Enterprise resource planning (ERP) technologies integrate all of the information within a single enterprise. Supply chain management (SCM) technologies, enhanced by Internet-based communications, foster cooperation. Workplaces enable companies to collaborate in "value webs" that provide better products and services to their customers along the product value chain and, ultimately, to consumers.

By closely linking each entity's business processes with the participants in those processes, workplaces and multi-party business hubs (marketplaces/exchanges) make greater collaboration possible. Today, the development of marketplaces accessed via workplaces is aimed at collaboration among communities of enterprises, their business partners, and all interested parties throughout their organizations.

PHASE I: INTEGRATION THROUGH ENTERPRISE RESOURCE PLANNING

Integration reduces costs as processes become standardized, predictable, and streamlined. By fusing data to the actions they parallel, enterprise-centric ERP software tightly integrates all of the information and processes within an enterprise.

Integrating legacy systems requires comprehensive IT solutions and manual procedures. ERP provides real-time update and verification of company information and seamless integration to critical business processes. It standardizes on one central data model and one central process model and facilitates change through corporate-specific configuration. Outside integration to customers and suppliers occurs through point-to-point communication, using electronic data interchange (EDI) technology.

Implementing ERP may involve many structural changes that can require a huge initial investment. Optimizing processes and business functions requires system or configuration changes. Depending on its depth, change can have a large impact on the organizational structure and also be very costly. However, the initial investment streamlines business processes and greatly reduces costs—two prerequisites for staying in business.

An ERP implementation focuses on intra-enterprise business processes. E-business requires the addition of inter-enterprise collaboration.

PHASE 2: COOPERATION THROUGH SUPPLY CHAIN MANAGEMENT AND INTERNET-BASED COMMUNICATION

Cooperation reduces costs and increases the speed with which processes can be carried out throughout the extended enterprise and across the product's value chain. Exercising central control over business processes spanning several enterprises generates the same benefits from SCM that ERP delivers: Inter-enterprise business processes are streamlined and front- and back-office process data are linked. Cooperation increases cross-department communication and optimizes supply chain life cycles.

Cooperation requires inter-enterprise central planning and careful attention to supply-chain management. The latter involves creating seamless business processes across company boundaries and linking, through IT, all mission-critical business processes between companies. The result is standardization and central control, change that is facilitated by industry-specific system configuration, and strong outside integration of selected business processes.

EDI—which facilitated one-to-one communication between supplier and purchaser and increased communication between the front and back offices of individual enterprises—was among the first technologies to foster cooperation. ERP technologies provided a much-needed backbone, making possible the development of other technologies to manage the supply chain. "Cooperative" technologies like SCM are intended to supplement, not to replace ERP. However, unless all of the players across the extended enterprise use very similar ERP packages and align their business processes to a common standard, much extra effort has to be made to link together all of the players in the extended enterprise.

While usage varies, cooperative technology is still based on strict integration rules. Community-building and relationship-building processes happen outside of the system. Moreover, while the technology is effective, it cannot dictate how individuals interact with each other or with virtual entities that individuals use to acquire data or information, that is, with workplaces or marketplaces.

PHASE 3: COLLABORATION THROUGH ADVANCED TECHNOLOGIES

A major difference between cooperation and collaboration is that while both can occur in near real time, collaboration involves ad-hoc, multi-directional flows of data and information rather than a sequential, linear flow. Collaborative technology allows for open, flexible integration within business communities. Collaborative tools are flexible and based on workflows rather than rigid and based on processes. On the one hand, they provide better support for how individuals actually carry out the tasks necessary to support existing business processes. On the other hand, they allow for end-to-end rather than partial coverage of key business processes. These tools are user- and role-centric, rather than business-process centric. Collaborative technology allows for the human spontaneity and unpredictability that occur within chaotic business processes—that is, those based on individual and community-based relationships.

Collaborative technology—the next step in the e-business technology revolution—is the cornerstone of the workplace. It imposes a kind of centralized control over the information exchanged among all of the players in the value chain. It increases revenue generation by fostering close relationships among customers, end-use consumers, and other members of the value web who work together to provide the best possible products and services.

Unlike EDI, which enables only tightly coupled one-to-one messaging, collaborative technology also makes possible one-to-many and many-to-many communication. With current Internet technologies, messages can be moved back and forth in real time. Without the right technology, such communication is chaotic, that is, uncontrolled and unstructured. However, workplace technology enables the user to consolidate, collate, and route communication to the appropriate party in the appropriate enterprise.

THE WORKPLACE: THE ULTIMATE COLLABORATIVE TOOL

Used in conjunction with other advanced technologies, workplaces open up new collaboration opportunities for a company. When workplaces extend beyond the boundaries of an individual company to involve its customers, suppliers, and business partners, they facilitate collaboration and information sharing across multiple enterprises.

Workplaces can handle e-business transactions, provide information on already-purchased goods or services and real-time order tracking, and suggest value-added opportunities based on a customer's personal profile. Suppliers might utilize the workplace to manage inventory at the production site in real time and to perform collaborative planning for future demand. Groups within the enterprise can better use in-house information to reduce costs and make processes user centric.

Individuals Are Key

The underlying premise of the new workplace paradigm is this: Individuals are key to business success. In the world of e-business, individuals are increasingly responsible for maintaining relationships with people at companies that collaborate with their employer.

Computers in business have increasingly enabled companies to integrate functions, activities, and processes, giving each individual working within a company a personal view of the enterprise, the extended enterprise of affiliated business partners, and the relationships among those entities. However, the information needed to perform transactions and manage relationships differs according to each individual's role in the company. Obviously, the information a CFO needs differs from that required by a sales manager or a field technician.

Workplaces solve that problem by offering individual, role-based front ends customized to the tasks associated with specific jobs. They provide the best means of satisfying both personal and corporate needs, and enable all workers to acquire the information, applications, and services they need to perform their specific roles.

Workplaces Empower Individuals

More and more, employees are being empowered to directly participate in a growing number of collaborative business processes. The wealth of information, applications, and services available to employees from a company's internal systems and from external providers is increasing rapidly. Without an integrated view of this ever-changing environment—a personalized workplace for all the roles in which an individual may act—employees can easily become overwhelmed. Furthermore, the value that can be derived from applications and information technology is limited.

Workplaces are doors through which working individuals can access a variety of content, including information and applications about businesses and the industries and markets in which they operate. They can also enable access to services that companies require in order to operate effectively. Taken together, all workplaces used by individuals who interact with a particular enterprise —employees, suppliers, customers, and other business partners— form a community platform. Through the workplace, all individuals who participate in company-related activities become part of the extended virtual organization and can access data and information pertinent to all of the business ecosystems that surround any company.

While a workplace contains views specific to all of an organization's roles, each individual's workplace front end is specific to his or her role and provides access only to information, applications, and services that support that role. The workplace delivers the convenience of navigation among the tools workers need in order to participate in an increasing number of business processes. Utilizing the concept of self-service, the workplace lets people focus on the business and forget about the technology. Users no longer have to worry about where an application's components reside, about which user name or password to use, or about how to move in context from one tool to another without having to re-key data. Also, they do not have to wade through large amounts of data to get to the key information they need. Figure 1.1 illustrates a disjointed view of the information, applications, and services an individual needs to accomplish necessary tasks during a workday; Figure 1.2 illustrates a unified view of these items. Only with a workplace, complete with a role-based workplace front end, is such unity possible.

BUILDING UP, NOT REPLACING

Collaborative technologies like the workplace blur the boundaries that define the enterprise, its supply-chain partners and its customers, and those that define ERP, customer relationship management (CRM), and SCM technologies. However, in a collaborative world, these technologies have not become obsolete. Rather, they are the cornerstones and solid foundation for successful e-business implementation. Workplace and other collaborative technologies provide the missing pieces to individuals who participate in both new and existing business processes.

Figure 1.1   Disjointed View

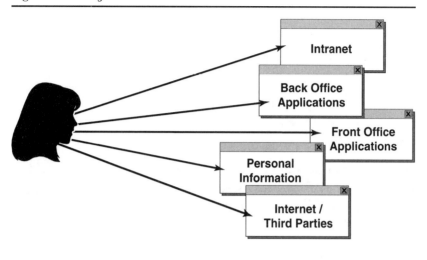

Figure 1.2   Unified View

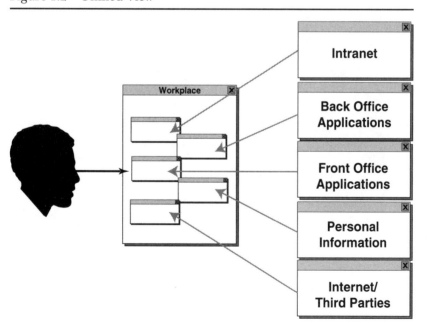

Figure 1.3   Traditional Supply Chain

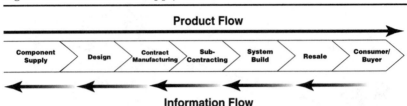

VALUE WEBS

When integration and even cooperation held sway in the world of business, enterprises were linked together in a traditional supply chain (Figure 1.3). In a collaborative business world peopled by workplace empowered employees, groups of suppliers and customers create integrated, multi-enterprise value webs (Figure 1.4).

In a traditional supply chain, demand and supply are loosely linked. In a value web, the response to supply or demand signals is rapid. In a supply chain, the flow of information is uni-directional

Figure 1.4   Integrated Value Web

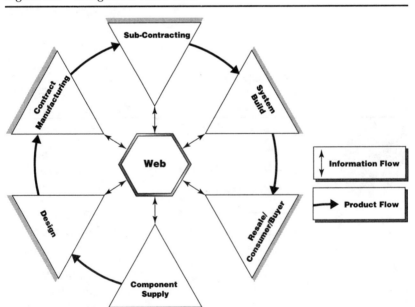

and disjointed. In a value web, information moves bi-directionally. In a supply chain, companies are connected by EDI and the mode of connectivity among entities is undifferentiated. In a value-web, individualized workplace connectivity fosters collaboration. In a supply chain, the ability to match supply and demand is limited. In a value web, tools are available to match supply and demand across multiple enterprises.

FROM COOPERATION TO COLLABORATION: RECONCILIATION IN THE OIL INDUSTRY

Oil companies work *cooperatively* all the time. During the course of any month, one company short of crude oil for refining or short of a particular product category can expect assistance from another. There is no invoicing for this trade, just a note of confirmation issued at the time of delivery. At the end of the month, these deliveries must be reconciled and priced appropriately.

This current process seems collaborative, but information technology support is only cooperative. Working on the honor system, the receiving company accepts the sending company's assertion that delivery was made on a particular day and settles the bill at the end of the month. Later on, someone compares the company's receipts with the sending company's deliveries. This process, done by hand, is tedious and must be performed by each company that engaged in any activity, either sending or receiving product.

The *collaborative* process must be totally supported by a similarly collaborative e-business infrastructure. An independent third party collects the notes of delivery. At the end of the month, an automated, rule-based clearing process for all of the bills clears the transactions. The workplace also supports the parties to the transactions as they work together collaboratively to clear the accounts. The current status of transactions that are in dispute is transparent to all parties. The collaborative process is much faster and more responsive. Many companies work together as if they were one.

2

People Matter:
The Human Dimension

While few would deny that technology is the main driver of change in business and society, technological change for many people is a fearsome thing. Part of that fear may result from a handful of misconceptions about technology, for example, that technology threatens jobs and personal control. There is also a concern that technology does not add value. Dispelling those fears means acknowledging that they contain a grain of truth and then offering an alternative scenario that positions technology in its proper role—as the servant of those who use it.

FEAR OF TECHNOLOGY IN BUSINESS
AND IN POPULAR CULTURE

Today's advanced technologies derive from industrial automation and have often carried with them the notion that computers are meant to replace people. For employees of large companies, whether production or support employees, this created a persistent fear that technology implementation meant job loss for the short term and fewer jobs in the future. Workers' uneasiness concerning the adoption of technology created a difficult environment in which to bring about change. This was true not only in the 1960s and 1970s, but even throughout the 1980s and 1990s.

Since the 1960s, the same idea has figured prominently in popular culture. For example, at the 1964 World's Fair in New

York, the General Electric Company hosted the GE Theater pavilion, a theater-in-the-round in which audiences sat in four pie-shaped auditoriums. The stage rotated, presenting four vignettes. The earliest involved the invention of the electric light bulb and the telephone. The final posited a vision of the future, in which machines would take over many mundane household chores.

Similar scenarios formed the basis of some television shows of the period. An animated program called *The Jetsons*, for example, featured an early twenty-first century family that resided in a space-pod community on Earth, where people traveled in craft that hovered over the ground and communicated with others on video phones that automatically activated whenever a person thought he or she wanted to speak to someone else. In this program, artificial intelligence is portrayed as being better than the human kind.

While fear of technology still exists today, it is dissipating. The current pervasiveness of technology in business and popular culture has caused many people to revise their vision of an idyllic world: The little house in the country may still be a desirable goal for many, but more often than not, that little country house of fantasy is now outfitted with a fast internet connection, a television satellite dish, and a sophisticated computerized fire and intruder alarm. Interestingly, such a vision places the human being at the center of the technology, not the other way around.

MOVING FROM FEAR TO EMPOWERMENT

While it's easy to view technology as dehumanizing, in the world of the workplace, the human dimension is more important than ever before. Despite rapid technological advances, the business world is changing from one in which the machine *constrains* people to one in which the machine *supports* people in executing their work. In this new world, the historic constraints of software—that it is centralized, complex, and rigid around one output—no longer limit the vision of how work can be accomplished and how organizational change can occur. In a world where each individual can change his or her workplace, and thus change the way he or she accomplishes work, companies can more economically bring about change and workers cease to fear it. In this world, organizational change is truly an ongoing reality, not something that happens in fits and starts as new systems are implemented or processes reengineered.

Employees who once viewed their relationship with computers as one in which the desired output drives their input, now think of it as one in which their input informs the output. They no longer need to fear technology-centric processes and systems. Rather, they can hope to be liberated by people-centric technologies.

FROM STATIC TO DYNAMIC PROCESSES AND SYSTEMS

Once, business was defined by static functions, processes, and systems, and individuals worked as best as they could within them. Today, business is defined by dynamic systems and processes, and workers adapt those systems and processes to the ways in which tasks need to be performed in order to meet customer needs.

Figure 2.1 illustrates how people have related to the processes and systems with which they work during three different time

Figure 2.1   People Are Most Important in the Workplace

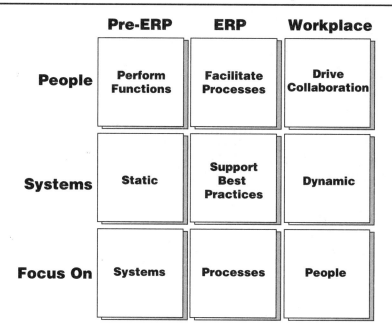

	Pre-ERP	ERP	Workplace
People	Perform Functions	Facilitate Processes	Drive Collaboration
Systems	Static	Support Best Practices	Dynamic
Focus On	Systems	Processes	People

periods: The earliest era predates enterprise resource planning (ERP) software. This is followed by an era when ERP-dominated systems thinking. The third era is today's new world of the workplace.

In a world of flexible processes, people can easily personalize their workplaces. This does not mean that processes have become anarchic, but it does mean that individuals can "tweak" the system and make minor adjustments in the processes to add efficiencies or increase effectiveness.

LOOKING BACK

Until the 1980s, most business workflow and many non-critical processes were completely manual. Processes that involved large volumes of transactions were accomplished using batch-oriented systems. Most software was custom written, and only a few packaged solutions existed. The first packages were database management solutions developed in the late 1970s and early 1980s. In the early 1980s, desktop computing arrived, as did the first desktop spreadsheet software. The IT departments of most corporations tried to keep desktop computers out of their companies—the first people who brought their home PCs to work were known as "desktop guerrillas." These individuals automated their own work processes based on their own unique requirements. They calculated data on spreadsheets, but then had to reenter their conclusions into the batch system. No real information sharing existed. A new employee who needed it had either to get the former employee's actual desktop spreadsheet or to create a new one.

Generally, until the mid- and even late 1990s, most working individuals had poor PC skills. A system implementation meant that a lot of people would need to learn a drastically new and different skill set. For many years, training programs for these skills were almost nonexistent.

ERP BEGINS TO CONNECT PEOPLE TO SYSTEMS

Bruce Sterling, co-founder of the Electronic Frontier Foundation, argues that: "Computing isn't thinking. We need to stop trying to get computers to think, and get serious about computing." The developers of ERP were thinking along the same lines. They were not interested in computer systems replacing people's ability to think, but in their ability to eliminate tedious but often complex computational chores. ERP sought to incorporate the best practice for performing particular tasks involved in many processes.

ERP did connect with individuals in that processes became much more transparent. The system enabled people to go beyond the immediate set of tasks they needed to perform in order to do their jobs and take advantage of information available across the enterprise. As problems were solved, some people were able to see how the solution helped to define the next opportunity.

ERP had major value added for large companies that daily moved huge volumes of transactional data across the enterprise. But workers who actually performed the tasks had no input in deciding where value would be pursued. In other words, the computer was still driving the business and employees were being pulled along in its wake. And ERP systems had other drawbacks; many people found them hard to learn and to use. Workers had to learn about the new processes in order to get value out of the ERP system. This learning was formal, time consuming, and expensive, but if it didn't take place, the company didn't derive value from the expensive ERP implementation. However, people had to deal with a larger part of the process than before, and they had to learn more than before. The increased responsibility that accompanied dealing with a larger part of the process did give some people a feeling of greater satisfaction in their roles.

FROM USER TO MASTER

In its capacity as a tool that quickly and cheaply moves information, applications, and services to individuals who have electronic access to company information, the Internet has redefined the way individuals work with computer systems.

Before the widespread availability of the Internet, individuals utilizing a company's computer systems were users who were dominated by the machine (hardware) and the system (software). They performed essentially the same set of business tasks on the system that they previously had performed manually. For example, an account payable was still an account payable; the computer simply consolidated many steps formerly performed manually into a single set of computations and automatic postings and then generated the necessary forms that had previously been hand written or typed. Processes were clearly defined and information technology supported them. Complex and static IT systems were designed to make processes more efficient by taking care of many of the more mundane manual tasks associated with transaction processing.

When ERP software arrived on the scene, its great virtues included its ability to codify information in order to eliminate even more of the manual data crunching and to post transactional information to all parties affected by a single transaction. In order to maximize ERP's effectiveness, however, processes had to be reengineered to conform to best practices. Once this was accomplished, the standard software solutions embedded in ERP easily replaced much human effort.

But, despite obvious improvements, the ERP solution presented two problems. First, the new processes and the systems designed to support them were equally as static as the old ones. To be sure, they improved process efficiency, but they still could not be adapted easily to customer-driven desires. Second, and more important from a human perspective, people were forced to make major adjustments to the way they worked in order to utilize the new system and to receive from it all of the promised business advantages. These adjustments were neither natural nor intuitive. Once again, people were being forced to fit their activities and the way they performed tasks into pre-defined processes established to achieve maximum efficiency from the computer system.

Workplace-based systems are causing dramatic change. Once again the person has risen in importance. No longer is he or she merely a system user, forced to adapt behavior to the requirements of the machine. Rather, individuals are the masters of their workplaces, able to manipulate them in order to receive the information, applications, and services they need to perform their daily tasks.

With the workplace, each individual begins with a generic set of information, applications, and services that is based on an equally generic "role" that pre-defines the person's responsibilities within the company. The individual, working with company management, can then modify and further refine the definition of that role, and by doing so, add to the workplace other sources of information, applications, and services.

With access to the company's systems and to the Internet through the workplace, workers become masters of the machine. They can draw upon the full range of the system's functionality to access whatever they need for the tasks they must perform. They do not become bogged down in the unwanted and unnecessary complexity that results when systems presented material to individuals only in one way.

DESIGN CONCEPTS

In order for people to enjoy working with their computer-based workplace, the system must be designed from a human, rather than a system-architecture perspective. To accomplish this, system designers have to look at how people perform their activities and tasks and design the software to facilitate these natural work rhythms. The software must also be easy to learn. Navigation complexities are the bane of many ERP and other mainframe-based or client-server corporate systems. Workplace software should be simple to navigate and easy to adapt to people's needs.

Visualization is important. For software to be enjoyable, the screens it generates must be appealing to the eye. Screen design should direct the eye to important elements and intuitively alert the brain to the navigational flow. The tone of the design should be soft rather than garish, with important elements highlighted. In addition, the screen should include multiple fields so that an individual has to go through fewer steps to access data. In short, a person should know where to go and how to get there without having to puzzle it out. A good design can accomplish this.

A well-designed workplace will also affect the way applications are designed and redesigned in the future. Software designers will have to create applications that are "aware" they are being run in a workplace environment. For example, navigation between applications accessed via the workplace must be easy and intuitive.

KNOWLEDGE IS POWER

Information is a strategic resource. But using information strategically requires a clear vision of the human dimensions of information use. Different companies have different knowledge use cultures. Some have an environment that might be called technocratic utopianism, where all of a company's information assets are organized and categorized rigidly, with heavy emphasis on technological solutions. In other companies, anarchy reigns, and each individual is left to obtain and manage his or her own information in a haphazard way.

Some companies have a feudal knowledge culture, where information is managed by individual business unit or function and only limited information is reported to the corporation at large. Others are more like a monarchy, where necessary information and reporting structures are defined by the company's leaders, who rarely share the information after collecting it.

Finally, knowledge federalism can prevail, where information management is based on consensus and negotiation about the key information elements and information reporting structures within the company.

In the world of static systems, rigid processes, and slow change, knowledge was often hoarded as a way of maintaining power. In the world of workplace systems, each individual must share information with others in order to derive full value from the tool and in order to carry out all of his or her activities in a way that provides service to customers and ultimately value to shareholders.

Increasing Flexibility

The Internet has made it necessary that companies be able quickly to adapt processes to new and ever-changing customer desires and market requirements. Therefore, employees too, must have flexibility in how they carry out their tasks. Such flexibility is impeded if systems underlying a company's business processes are fixed and rigid. To be poised to respond to new and perhaps unforeseen demands, both companies and the individuals that work within them must be capable of quickly responding to change within the system or even of adding new systems to support new demands upon existing business processes.

Such flexibility is possible partly because of the availability of application service providers (ASPs) who maintain and manage system applications. It is also due in part to the availability of the Internet as a means of gaining quick access to new sources of information, applications, and services. Because of these new tools, if a company finds that it must add a new system in order to respond to new customer, supplier, or business partner requirements, it no longer has to purchase the system and install it on its computers, code all of its company information on the software, and then train users. Today, a new system can be "rented" from an ASP on a per-transaction, per-desktop, or monthly basis. The ASP is responsible for maintaining both the application and the company-specific data within it. Those who must utilize this application need only learn how to get to it through the ASP's front-end and the workplace's Web browser.

EVERY INDIVIDUAL CAN BE A SYSTEM INTEGRATOR

With more access to and control over knowledge, and with increased flexibility, all workers today can create, execute, and be accountable for processes. Computers are tools used for getting the work done within those processes. Many low-skilled activities within business processes have become automated. Today's jobs require highly skilled employees who can keep track of complex processes while participating in and even creating constant change.

The emphasis has shifted from understanding a static best practice to continuous learning. Individuals are no longer limited by having to use best-practice configurations within a computer system. These configurations are only a starting point. Individuals are asked to redefine best practices on the fly, reconfigure the system, and communicate their knowledge to others so the new best practice can be immediately institutionalized. Workers today are faced with a new reality, quite different from the ideal world of an artificial system construct. To operate effectively within this new reality, each individual will have to be able to navigate between configured best practice and the appropriate workflow.

Individuals, therefore, require access to the tools they need to undertake continuous learning, to implement change, and to locate the best information and applications and the services to support them. People also need access to the Internet, planning optimization tools, data warehouses, and knowledge management tools. Very soon, most system configuration change will be implemented not by a system administrator, but by an individual who has the ability to customize his or her individual workplace.

THE WORKPLACE PUTS PEOPLE IN CONTROL

With a workplace, individuals have access to the information, applications, and services they need to perform their immediate tasks through a flexible system that they can reconfigure to meet their ever-changing definition of best practice. This is especially important in an environment where more and more individuals are knowledge workers. Such workers are willing, able, and even eager to take more responsibility for managing the way in which they interact with information, applications, and services. Where knowledge work dominates, the value of information increases in proportion to the number of people who possess it.

The workplace provides ease of access to many systems, allowing an individual to see the entire process across enterprise lines. As data entry and manipulation become more and more automated, people are freer to take on work that involves decision support and decision making, in short, work that has strategic impact.

We began this chapter by commenting on the dehumanizing aspects of technology. We end it with the workplace—technology that puts the human being solidly back in control.

MANAGING COMPLEXITY

The beauty of the workplace is that it simplifies the way information, applications, and services are delivered to each individual, while at the same time increasing the richness of the material an individual receives. While the system is, in fact, more complex technically than ever before, most of the increased complexity is not apparent to the person using the system, a situation that parallels the development of other technologies. Consider, for example, the technological development of airplanes, cameras, or, for that matter, automobiles.

From the 1920s to the 1960s, the number of systems a pilot needed to track in order to fly a plane increased to over 600. Engineers continuously added systems in the belief that the more parameters were measured, the more control the pilot had. In reality, as pilots came to realize, having to track over 600 systems was not only impractical, but potentially dangerous. Since the 1960s, the number of systems a pilot actually tracks has been greatly reduced. The variables are still measured by systems, but the pilot has fewer actual controls to monitor.

With regard to the camera, today a simple 35-millimeter automatic-focus camera with a zoom lens does as much as a 1960s vintage professional-model camera but without the dozens of adjustments the photographer had to make. With respect to automobiles, a mechanic today needs upward of $100,000 in computer-aided diagnostic tools. The driver, however, only needs to monitor engine temperature, fuel level, and oil pressure.

3

Value Proposition for E-Business and Workplaces

Before creating a workplace that includes access to disparate internal systems and external sources of information and applications, some attempt must be made to calculate the return on the investment. To do this, it is necessary for company leaders to construct a business case that clearly explains how the effort will enhance corporate value.

A business case is more than just a cost justification for the CFO's benefit. A business case provides those who will implement a project or change effort—and those who will manage the resulting operations—with a baseline of hoped-for and/or anticipated results against which to measure progress. A properly constructed business case should cover both the financial and non-financial performance metrics against which to measure the implementation.

In large part, this chapter discusses the value proposition for e-business. We can extend these concepts to the workplace. The workplace is an integral part of e-business, because much of the value of e-business is derived from increasingly collaborative relationships. E-business needs the workplace and the workplace needs e-business. Both in tandem provide maximum value.*

---

*PricewaterhouseCoopers consultants have articulated the business case for e-business in two previous books: Martin V. Deise, Conrad Nowikow, Patrick King, and Amy Wright, *Executive's Guide to E-Business: From Tactics to Strategy* (New York: John Wiley & Sons, 2000), and Grant Norris, James R. Hurley, Kenneth M. Hartley, John R. Dunleavy, and John D. Balls, *E-Business and ERP: Transforming the Enterprise* (New York: John Wiley & Sons, 2000).

E-BUSINESS ENHANCES REVENUE *AND* REDUCES COSTS

While enterprise resource planning (ERP) is inward looking—about integrating the transactional data and process information within a company—e-business is outward looking—about connecting to and communicating with customers, suppliers, and business partners.

The justification for implementing ERP is that it cuts costs. Integrated data increases process efficiency. At the same time, it reduces transaction costs, information management costs with respect to the hardware, software, and staff necessary to maintain legacy systems, and staff-training costs over time as staff become more "change ready." By eliminating much of the tedium and opportunity for error associated with reentering data into multiple systems, ERP streamlines operations, simplifies order management, and consolidates many procurement activities. It provides both financial consolidation and technology consistency, and reduces system maintenance costs. The savings associated with many of these improvements can be easily quantified—either people are able to do more work or fewer people are needed to do the same amount of work.

The financial benefits of e-business, however, are much harder to quantify because e-business is about establishing new kinds of relationships with parties outside the company, including customers in the distribution channel and end-use consumers, suppliers and business partners, and third-party service providers. While it is possible to quantify the savings provided by establishing e-business links with suppliers, it is much more difficult to quantify the impact e-business has on a company's "sell side" customer relationship management processes.

KEY E-BUSINESS BENEFITS

In e-business, knowledge replaces much machinery and inventory. Relationships with participants up and down the value chain replace much of the management infrastructure necessary to make one-off purchases and sales. And rapid transfer of knowledge across corporate boundaries replaces much of the face-to-face communication prevalent in non-e-business transactions.

E-business increases revenues by improving each of the four variables that affect customer value:

1. *Service goes up.* E-business improves customer service in a number of ways. It provides interactive personalized service, speed and accuracy, enhanced ability to track and measure capability, and 24×7 availability.
2. *Price goes down.* With price transparency, auctions, volume aggregation, and pay-per-use, e-business customers are finding prices for goods and services continuously falling.
3. *Quality goes up.* Quality in e-business is more than just the quality of the underlying good or service. It is also the quality of the transaction and, indeed, of the entire customer relationship. With e-business, a company can provide a customized experience for different groups of customers or even for an individual customer.
4. *Fulfillment time goes down.* E-business reduces the time that transpires from initial customer order to delivery. This is partially accomplished by Web-based systems that allow for customer configuration, and partially by back-end supply chain management systems that tie together all of the participants in the e-business supply chain.

ACHIEVING BUSINESS VALUE

Workplaces help companies attain business value by both reducing costs and enhancing revenues for the companies that use them. Figure 3.1 illustrates how the benefits of a workplace—reduced cost of information technology, reduced cost of business processes, and increased revenues—more than make up for a company's investment in a workplace system.

Figure 3.2 describes the business value equation. While the total cost of ownership is tangible and can be calculated, the total benefits of ownership are both intangible and tangible. Therefore the business value generated is not simply an amount of cash.

The benefits of a workplace are both operational and strategic. Operational benefits are realized by automating manual processes, while retaining the processes themselves. Strategic benefits are

Figure 3.1   Effects of a Workplace

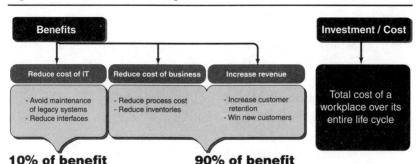

realized by exploiting the opportunities offered by information technology to redesign ways of doing business and to create new business models (e.g., Web selling). Operational benefits are easier to identify than strategic benefits.

Cost Reduction: A Lower Cost of Ownership

Workplaces lower the cost of ownership for technology—both hardware and software. With workplace technology, applications reside on a server rather than on each individual's PC. Individuals access applications through their customized workplace front ends and work within them comfortably and naturally. The only software actually installed on the desktop is a standard Web browser.

Figure 3.2   Business Value Equation

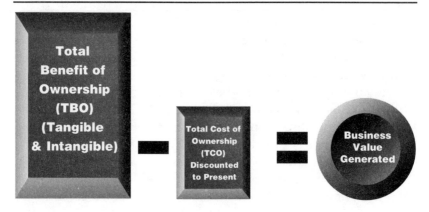

The workplace provides unified access to all applications. Since users have access to these applications through the browser, they need not concern themselves about where each application resides. The hosting of applications—either internally or externally—is completely transparent to the user. In addition, less software on the desktop means lower installation and maintenance costs and eliminates the need to upgrade hardware to run increasingly sophisticated computer programs. Workplace browsers and intuitive interfaces also eliminate the need to perform some training on specific applications.

Revenue Enhancement: Productivity, Reach, and Relationships

Workplaces enhance revenues by increasing productivity, extending reach, and enabling the formation of collaborative relationships.

Increasing Productivity

In the standard working environment, processes are decomposed into tasks and activities. The workplace environment builds from individual roles to business processes, resulting in higher productivity. By eliminating non-value-added steps, individuals are able to perform their work in a more intuitive way, thereby achieving a better understanding of how their work fits into business processes to create value. In addition, because only the relevant information and applications are presented in each individual workplace front end, users no longer need to search for relevant information. The workplace consolidates the various sources of information, applications, and services, eliminating the time-consuming steps of logging in and out of each system individually.

Access to multiple sources of information accelerates learning and information gathering. Easy access to company policies, procedures, and process documentation means that time-critical information can be pushed out to the workplaces. A single place for all vital information ensures effective knowledge management. In turn, improved knowledge management leads to more effective decision making, which enhances the value of intangible assets.

Workplace users can navigate easily among different applications. With drag and relate technology, for instance, they can combine material from various sources in a way that is most natural.

Navigational tools designed by the particular provider of workplace technology further enhance ease of use and speed.

While electronic workflow is pulled together at the business process level, it is maintained at the presentation level. Each individual, therefore, is better able to understand how his or her actions fit in with the actions of his or her co-workers. Work output created by actions undertaken in one role becomes the input for actions undertaken in another. The workplace, using the push concept, immediately notifies the role player of the actions taken and applicable alerts are constantly updated for all relevant roles.

An example will help to clarify this process. Let's say that a customer requests maintenance. The request is received and forwarded to maintenance scheduling. This work is then ranked against all other requests, given a priority status, and, based on availability, assigned to a field service engineer. The field service engineer who receives the request uses his workplace to determine what tools and supplies are needed and whether they are in stock. He validates that the supplies are on hand and schedules the work using software in the workplace to optimize his route based on all required stops and transit time from point to point. The field service engineer sets an appointment time, which the customer validates. When on site, he performs the maintenance and closes the job ticket. The closed ticket is automatically routed to customer billing, and an invoice is generated on the next invoice process run.

Faster information retrieval rates and faster response time to the critical business information that management pushes to individuals' workplaces increases productivity by improving the quality and timeliness of decision making and of responding to customer/business partner/colleague queries. A worker can, perhaps, save 15 minutes each day because of easier and more logically organized access to the information, applications, and services he or she needs to do a job. While 15 minutes might not seem like much, at the end of a year, they amount to 7 to 10 productive work days for each individual.

While speed and ease of use are important, they do not take precedence over security. Workplaces provide these benefits without sacrificing security. Single sign-on, role-based authorization to obtain particular information, data encryption, secure business document exchange with digital signature, and central administration protect corporate assets on the workplace. (We discuss security in greater depth in Chapter 8.)

Extending Reach

A company can extend its reach by creating workplaces for non-employees such as key suppliers, design collaborators, logistics providers, distribution partners, or key customers. Critical business information, applications, or services can be pushed out to everyone who utilizes the workplace through various alert mechanisms that attract users' attention no matter where they are within the workplace environment.

Building Collaborative Relationships

E-business is less about technology and more about relationships. Using workplaces, companies can develop focused and tightly linked relationships with key business partners along the value chain.

By providing business partners access to the workplace, companies can unleash value in a number of ways. For example, they can reduce inter-enterprise business process cycle time, enhance information sharing across company boundaries, and reduce partner support time and cost by providing business partners with self service access to information, applications, and services. In addition, sharing applications allows for closer collaboration on product design, production planning, and customer relationship management.

Collaborative relationships are not limited to business partners. They include those formed among individuals who work together in the workplace. When individuals collaborate, either inside or outside the company, their combined productivity increases geometrically—that is, the increased productivity of one individual is multiplied by the increased productivity of another. (We cover in detail this effect on increased productivity in Chapter 7 as part of our discussion of collaborative planning and collaborative design.)

EMPLOYEES BENEFIT FROM THE WORKPLACE

As well as providing macro corporate benefits, the workplace delivers benefits to individual employees. The ability to personalize and customize the workplace not only gives employees ease of access to the information, applications, and services they need to perform their jobs, but also can make their work more satisfying. Understanding their roles helps employees see how their actions fit into the key processes that produce value for customers and, by extension, value for shareholders. And, role definitions can be extended if employees wish to broaden the area of activities within which they take part or over which they have control. In addition, workplace technology allows in-office employees, telecommuters, and those who are on the road to work together seamlessly. An individual's location is immaterial to the way he or she interacts with the workplace or with others utilizing it.

With the workplace, employees have the ability to deal with certain personal matters, thereby increasing well being and improving overall job performance. For example, the workplace empowers employees to perform such tasks as checking the status of their retirement investments, or making adjustments to their benefits. They can also use the workplace to take charge of career building by, for example, linking their personal development plans to Web-based education and training.

Because the workplace allows any employee to see only those transactions for which his or her role is responsible, it streamlines the workflow associated with that role. This creates a work environment that is far more intuitive than one that requires employees to seek out multiple applications to get the job done. With push technology, employees can respond more quickly to critical changes in workflow and react more quickly to input from customers, business partners, or colleagues. The employee does not have to check continuously for the delivery of desired inputs from others involved in the process; they are automatically sent to his or her workplace.

As a tool in the world of mobile computing, the workplace liberates employees by freeing them from outdated work structures, especially in conjunction with the increasing array of wireless devices. Using the workplace, employees have the option of being productive at their jobs while also maintaining work and life structures that are appropriate to their situations. These can include telecommuting from home, working from a remote office site, or working from the road.

CUSTOMER VALUE EQUALS CORPORATE VALUE

The workplace gives companies the ability to respond faster and more completely to electronically connected customers. With self-service options, customers can find information, initiate orders, and check status without placing serious demands on company staff. The customer accesses information through a workplace just as the employee or collaborator does, and a host of relationship opportunities arises.

In reality, self-service puts more of the burden on the customer than is currently the case. However, the burden turns into a benefit when the customer feels more in control of the shape and form of the transaction—such as being able to configure a product to his or her specifications. Researchers, however, caution that the second generation of those willing to buy on the Web are requiring much more hand holding in the form of customer support than first-adopter Web-savvy shoppers, both among consumers and business clients. To mitigate potential customer anxiety, a community within the workplace environment can be created that optimizes communication to, from, and among customers. An added benefit is that such a community can be utilized for market research—for example, to track not only how customers are responding to current products and services, but also what products and services they would like in the future.

Customers also benefit from the host of value-adding services that can be delivered through a workplace, thereby improving customer satisfaction and cementing customer loyalty. For example, the workplace could include a customer-specific profile that expedites each customer's ordering process; or, it could direct customers to additional goods or services that have a tight affinity with those they have ordered. A customer, for example, ordering an automobile might be directed to collateral products and services such as insurance, financing, or maintenance plans. Using the workplace, customers can also express preferences for the way

Figure 3.3   Jump Starting Business Value with Workplaces

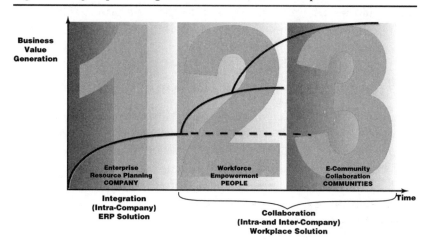

they wish to receive information in the future—e-mail, voice mail, fax, or hard copy mail.

Figure 3.3 illustrates how workplaces can jump start business value. While ERP systems focus on integrating intra-company systems and reducing costs, the workplace focuses on enhancing both intra-company and inter-company relationships.

BUILDING THE BUSINESS CASE

Building the business case for a workplace involves four steps:

1. *Identify potential cost savings and new revenues.* This includes performance improvement, potential collaborative arrangements, and more efficient purchasing.

2. *Identify participants and/or partners in the effort.* This involves determining the best-of-breed products and practices in each e-business model that might be adopted and quantifying the human aspects (both tangible and intangible) of the project.

3. *Assess the project parameters.* This involves estimating implementation costs, timetables, and time constraints imposed by market forces and other influences.

4. *Decide whether to pursue the project.* This involves determining the company's internal hurdle rate, matching costs to the business goals, identifying costs associated with human components, and determining the lost opportunity costs of not pursuing a project.

Identify Potential Cost Savings and New Revenues

In this step, a company tries to assess its e-business strategy, including its need and desire to collaborate with business partners. The company must also determine the tradeoffs it finds acceptable among the four primary variables of any e-business initiative—complexity, speed, cost, and functionality.

When these have been determined and understood, the project team can follow standard IT implementation procedures: assess the current state, create a vision for the desired future state, and map out a transformation process to get from here to there. This process includes identifying and assessing likely constraints and challenges, and finding tactical, quick-win opportunities (so-called low-hanging fruit).

Identify Participants and Partners

To identify potential partners and other participants in the e-business effort, a company should utilize what we refer to as the 7-C model (Figure 3.4). Each C implies a set of questions; answering these questions helps determine how many and what kinds of partners are necessary to the effort and how the company will interact with those partners.

The 7-C model helps to structure and organize information by creating a framework for discussions about e-business. It provides a starting point for formulating strategy, and for identifying relationships among issues. Broadly speaking, the seven Cs can be consolidated into three categories:

1. Strategic positioning, which includes community and content
2. Corporate strategy, which includes collaboration, competition, and company

Figure 3.4 The 7-C Model

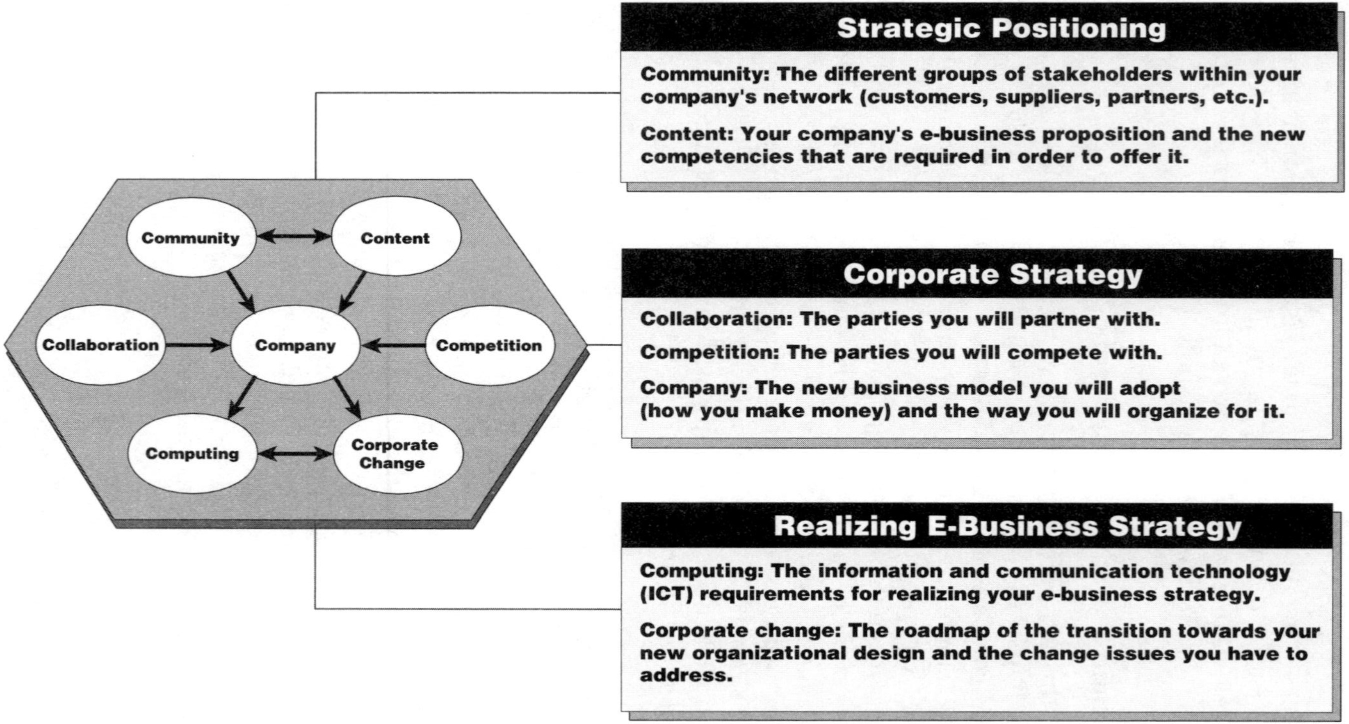
Community
Content
Collaboration
Company
Competition
Computing
Corporate Change
Strategic Positioning
Community: The different groups of stakeholders within your company's network (customers, suppliers, partners, etc.).
Content: Your company's e-business proposition and the new competencies that are required in order to offer it.
Corporate Strategy
Collaboration: The parties you will partner with.
Competition: The parties you will compete with.
Company: The new business model you will adopt (how you make money) and the way you will organize for it.
Realizing E-Business Strategy
Computing: The information and communication technology (ICT) requirements for realizing your e-business strategy.
Corporate change: The roadmap of the transition towards your new organizational design and the change issues you have to address.

3. E-business strategy, which includes computing and corporate change.

Strategic Positioning: Community and Content

Community addresses the different groups of stakeholders within a company and its network, including customers, suppliers, business partners, shareholders, and others.

The key questions to ask about community are:

- To what non-virtual community or communities does the company belong?
- What does this imply about the virtual community or communities of which the company should be a part in the connected world?
- Of what virtual community or communities should the company strive to be a part?
- How will this group act as a community? What are the common elements and what are the business drivers for members of the virtual community?
- What will be the dynamics of this desired virtual community? What will be the new value drivers?
- Where will customer value be created in the new community? Which member(s) will be best positioned?

Content addresses a company's e-business proposition and the new competencies that are required in order to offer it and refers to the value proposition it wishes to put forward. In order to determine a company's particular content proposition in an e-business environment, its current value and unique selling propositions, brands, and core competencies need to be assessed. The company then must envision how workplace technology can strengthen its ability to deliver on these value propositions, and determine if there are new propositions that the technology enables the company to offer to the market.

The key questions to ask about content are:

- What impact will e-business have on the company's present value to its current community?

- How will the company be positioned to participate in its desired virtual community?
- On what core competencies will the company base its position?
- What will be the company's customer-value strategy?

Corporate Strategy: Collaboration, Competition, and Company

Collaboration addresses the partnerships a company must form—that is, the set of strategic alliances—either industry-related or outside the company's industry—it must establish in order to provide its unique value proposition. A company needs to assess its current collaborators and envision what partnering needs are created in order to reach the desired community or communities.

The key questions to ask about collaboration are:

- Which activities the company engages in are considered core and which are non-core?
- Which non-core activities should be e-sourced?
- In the new community, and based on the company's desired content, with whom does the company need to collaborate?
- What are the risks and opportunities of working with these business partners?
- What alternative business partners are available for the company in the connected world?
- How will the company perform business partner management?

Competition addresses the changing competitive environment arising from e-business and how a company reacts to those changes. In the world of e-business, competitive challenges can come from many different directions: from traditional competitors within an industry, from competitors outside an industry whose products or processes can be brought into the industry, and from new dot.com companies that change the basis of competition by changing business processes. As well as assessing its current competitors, a company needs to envision from where new competitors will come, and on what basis they will compete.

The key questions to ask about the competitive environment are:

- What is the competitive situation in the connected world? Where will competitive advantage come from? And, in the connected world, is competitive advantage sustainable?
- What are the barriers to exiting the traditional competitive landscape?
- Which current competitor is best positioned to compete in the connected world?
- How will barriers to entry change? Can a particular e-business strategy increase the barriers to entry against competitors and help sustain competitive advantage?
- Is it necessary to collaborate with traditional competitors in order to employ any particular e-business strategy, for example, to raise entry barriers against newcomers?

Company addresses changing value drivers and the resulting new business model. Company refers to how an organization creates value from its e-business prospects, and the necessary organizational redesign that goes into such an effort. Analyzing the company aspect involves assessing the organization's current business model and organizational model, envisioning how the company's e-business effort will create value, and understanding what new organizational requirements will arise.

The key questions to ask about the company are:

- What will the company's value proposition be in the connected world?
- What are the new value drivers in the connected world?
- What is the impact of the connected world on shareholder value?
- How will employees be valued in the connected world?
- What are the new revenue and cost drivers in the connected world, and what impact will they have on the company's profitability?
- What business model should the company choose?
- What operational model should the company choose?

E-Business Strategy: Computing and Corporate Change

Computing addresses the information and communication technology a company requires in order to realize its value proposition and connect effectively with collaborators and communities. The company must assess its current information and technology capabilities and identify its short- and long-term technology priorities. Companies considering workplace technology, for example, do so because it provides a flexible basis on which to build other technology capabilities over time, such as mobile devices and broadband.

The key questions to ask about computing are:

- What technology trends are key to the business? Will e-business change or alter those trends?
- What impact will technology trends and new technologies have on the current business?
- How can the company best align its IT strategy with its business goals?
- Given the company's technology, how feasible is it to pursue e-business?
- Is it feasible to Web-enable the company's ERP systems? What would the impact be?

Corporate change refers to the process a company needs to follow to realize its e-business strategy and to manage change. A company needs to assess its current change management capabilities, envision the change management process it needs to go through, and decide on a realistic implementation approach. Research has shown that an e-business change strategy depends on organizational adaptability and incorporates a degree of uncertainty about the future.

The key questions to ask about corporate change are:

- What process will be needed to transform the company into one capable of prospering in the connected world?
- What change strategy will be employed to implement the project?

- What risks are involved in the move to the connected world?
- What is the financial and organizational cost of doing nothing?

Assess the Project Parameters

Estimate Cost and Time for Implementation

In 1999, Forrester Research suggested that workplaces should mimic consumer portals such as Yahoo! and Excite by developing in two stages. The first stage is to create a topic hierarchy that allows visitors to browse and search their way through the content; the second stage is to incorporate technology that visitors can use to create a customized home page (the analog of a workplace front-end page.) Forrester suggested that in the corporate world, a workplace first be populated with content (information) and then extended to make it easy for individuals to find and launch applications. According to Forrester, a large company might expect to spend about two years developing an appropriate content hierarchy at a cost of about $1.5 million, including a search server and the labor of corporate information specialists to populate the content site.

We believe, however, that individuals should be able to utilize their workplaces from the start to access not only information, but also applications and services. Development of content and applications should be simultaneous. Appropriate use of applications allows individuals to deal with content much more effectively in carrying out their day-to-day work-related tasks. Furthermore, to be effective, workplace software should function hand-in-hand with a company's ERP system, as well as with its order-entry and current Web site customer-facing front end.

Decide Whether To Pursue the Project

A business case provides a structured, repeatable process that, when applied to a proposed project, achieves measurable value. Companies must determine up front if the project is worth their investment of both human and financial capital. An organization's

Figure 3.5　Building the Benefits Case

Prerequisites

Trigger Events
- Enterprise not realizing full potential
- Loss of competitive advantage
- Sub-optimal process area performance

Input
- Executive interviews
- Public documents
- Previous business cases

Results

Output
- Diagnostic report
- Benefit realization risk assessment
- Business case (approved)

Outcome
- Understanding of enterprise (strategy value drivers, processes, etc.)
- Understanding of critical success factors
- Approval to develop benefits case and action plans further
- Commitment to benefits realization process
- Initial prioritization of opportunities with potential improvement ranges

internal hurdle rate will, in large measure, determine if a proposed project is worth the invested capital and if it will achieve a company's defined return over a specified period of time. The company must own the business case development timeline and deliverables.

Once a project has been initiated, the activities associated with building a business case provide additional data that can be used to substantiate further the project's benefits and to augment

Figure 3.6　Determining Targets, Priorities, and Projects

Prerequisites

Trigger Events
- Completed benefits realization diagnostic
- Project sponsor approval to continue benefits realization process

Input
- Industry or related process
- Benchmarks and best practices

Results

Output
- Documented business targets
- Prioritized list of potential project options and their associated benefit ranges
- Enterprise benefits baseline

Outcome
- Understanding of the financial impact of project scenarios
- Understanding of acceptable practices for benefit calculations
- Collaborative relationship with financial and management reporting staff
- Commitment to benefits realization process
- Initial prioritization of opportunities with potential improvement ranges

the case for additional analysis of future opportunities. The business case provides a range of options and helps to manage expectations with regard to expected benefits. It also helps management to prioritize opportunities to be developed during the next project phase and to decide if the project is worth pursuing. Figures 3.5 and 3.6 illustrate the activities involved in building an effective business case.

Furthermore, executive and senior management can use the business case to assess financial impacts linked to specific targets. It also provides financial perspective from which to assess the benefits developed early in the process. The business case should be updated regularly as the project progresses to ensure an ongoing and accurate documentation of financial benefits.

4

The Workplace
and Its Roles

In Shakespeare's play, *As You Like It*, the character Jaques speaks the following lines: "All the world's a stage./ And all the men and women merely players./ They have their exits and their entrances;/ And one man in his time plays many parts." While he could not have imagined it at the time, Shakespeare's words have extraordinary resonance for twenty-first century e-business and echo the concepts behind workplace technology. In that context, the "stage" is a company, or network of collaborating companies; the "players" are the individuals who work for those companies; and the "parts" are the roles that these individuals fulfill.

Extending the theater analogy is useful in clarifying the concept of roles. In a theater, each production requires different types of people to succeed: actors, stage crew, orchestra, audience. These people enter the theater from different doors according to the roles they fulfill. They see the same performance from different perspectives and rely on tools and information they need to perform their roles. For example, the lighting technician has cues but not a complete musical score; the audience has a synopsis but not a complete script. In many theaters people play multiple roles. Multiple roles require multiple sets of tools and information to fulfill them.

In business, the concept of roles is not new, but the current focus on roles is. Within a company, roles are pivotal to success. In

53

a business environment where more than ever before accountability is being pushed down through organizations, roles help determine an individual's accountability for particular tasks,
activities, or processes.

Roles are an outgrowth of and link people to business objectives and processes. When used to define a workplace, roles determine the information, applications, and services individuals can
access to help them accomplish what they need to do.

A role defines an activity set that an individual undertakes in
order to achieve a desired business objective. A role, rather than a
person, defines how a business process is fulfilled and, in turn,
how the business process leads to achieving a particular business
objective successfully. Processes become wrapped or embedded in
roles, and roles are responsible for ensuring that process tasks are
carried out. A role cannot truly exist without a business process or
many business processes that define a necessary activity set.

Why are roles more relevant and valuable today? Just as
processes enabled by technology become standardized, so too can
roles. This allows the development of workplaces based on roles.
Roles are also valuable because they become one entry point, one
building block, for communities of workers within companies.

Figure 4.1 illustrates the relationship between business objectives, processes, and roles in its simplest form. Figure 4.2 shows
a more complex relationship between business objectives,
processes, roles, and external influences.

A person assigned a role rarely performs all steps in a process.
Roles generally operate across a number of processes, performing
different steps in each based on an adequate segregation of duties
for the business.

Figure 4.1   Roles Meet Business Objectives (Simple)

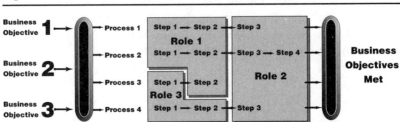

Figure 4.2   Roles Meet Business Objectives (Complex)

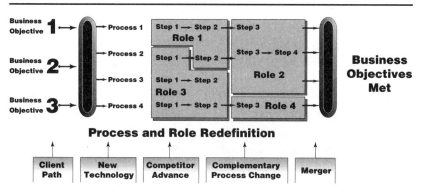

Processes are comprised of a number of components that utilize various information technology systems. A process is an input, transformation, and output function. Within the transformation portion of a process, an individual or many individuals are called on to use internal and external information, various applications, and external services. In the new business model, however, new technologies and mergers (where different processes for performing the same function are combined in one corporate reporting entity) are among the many factors redefining the way traditional business process steps are performed.

In the process-focused paradigm that has dominated business thinking since the 1980s, people's jobs have been defined by the processes they help carry out. But such a paradigm is too mechanical and depicts people's work as being secondary to the process. Conversely, in a role-focused business paradigm, processes become secondary to the people who carry them out and help attain business goals. Business is still organized around objectives and the outcomes necessary to achieve them, but today, roles are more important than processes.

CHARACTERISTICS OF ROLES

Roles are superior to processes as a means of organizing the fulfillment of business objectives. Unlike processes, roles are flexible and fluid and can be personalized easily by the individuals who fulfill them. Individuals empowered by roles can positively impact processes without having to go through a formal management structure or formal change procedures. This flexibility is especially important in the new economy, where business objectives are redefined quickly in reaction to outside stimuli on the business organism.

Accountability for fulfillment of business objectives is directly related to the complexity and dynamism of the role that carries out the activities, tasks, and processes necessary to achieve goals. At the same time, roles can grow and redefine themselves, even as they redefine the processes for which they are responsible.

Because employees often tailor the activities within their roles, a role's ability both to cover the required process activities and tasks and also to redefine processes as necessary is directly related to the accomplishment of business objectives. The emphasis moves from objectives based on function and process to more fluid role-and-process-based objectives.

Processes today need to be flexible enough to enable role players to adjust the processes and sub-processes in which they participate. In other words, role-playing individuals can change the flow of tasks under their control. When this occurs, all individuals who fill roles that interact in the process must be involved and their tasks adjusted accordingly.

More decentralized processes, such as employee self-service, might be changed by a group of individuals who use them. In most cases, however, an individual will not be allowed to change his or her own role, with the exception of tasks that are subject to workplace front-end personalization.

Knowledge of the role and of the most efficient way for it to carry out its process steps is kept within the role itself. Individuals performing roles enhance them over time as they discover better ways to carry out certain steps or new supporting information sources that are subsequently added to the workplace. Over time the workplace stimulates the development of "best practices" for roles and serves as a means of keeping them up to date.

ROLE COMPONENTS

To function in a dynamic business model, individuals working within roles require access to such pertinent components as:

- Internal and external systems and services
- Internal and external information, including internal policies and procedures and regulatory or industry information.

Access must be fast and available from a single location—through a single point of entry—in order to simplify for the user the actual complexity of the system landscape. Navigation from one component to another must be simple and easily customized. The workplace only offers the applications, information, and services that each particular individual needs to fulfill his or her role, regardless of where these originate.

A role can be built from a functional as well as a process perspective. The process perspective helps to reduce training because the role already reflects what a user should do in the order in which it should be done, and what information is typically needed to support these activities. These instructions are, in fact, business process knowledge stored within roles. For working individuals, roles also help make business control issues explicit by defining the information to which individuals or groups assigned to the same role have access.

Push Technology and Role Success

In the workplace, the individual uses the launch area to pull information, applications, or services he or she needs to perform specific tasks. These tasks might occur regularly or sporadically. Either the individual or the system can launch a certain application or access an information source, depending on the workflow.

Roles really create value for an organization when they are combined with information that is pushed to, rather than pulled by the individual. These information items go by many different names; SAP, for example, calls them MiniApps. Key performance indicators or time-critical alerts are pushed out to the individual's computer. Using drag and relate technology, an individual can take those messages that are useful, relevant, or important and move them into an appropriate folder on his or her workplace. Whenever an individual logs on to the workplace, the most current material relevant to his or her daily work appears in the push area for quick reference.

Other MiniApps can be pulled by the user whenever they are needed. Examples of pull-oriented MiniApps include calculators, currency converters, or translation assistants.

Function-Based Organizations

Common until the 1980s, function-based companies have a very rigid organizational structure. Individuals working for such companies are organized in silos according to the functions they fulfill—purchasing, accounting, manufacturing, logistics, and so on. Accountability for each functional organization's outcomes rests at the top of the functional hierarchy, and those in charge of functional areas report to corporate leadership. Such organizations take a function-based approach to business (e.g., telecommunications companies that only offer telephone service). Figure 4.3 illustrates a simple function-based organization.

The systems that help manage this type of organization emulate the organizational design. Menus are functional and modular and based on the system's functionality, not on the user's assigned access. In fact, most users are unable to gain access to 75 percent of the menu items displayed. A user has to fight through a lot of clutter in the menu in order to get to what he or she needs to complete tasks and activities and to fulfill his or her business objectives. For example, during creation of a sales order, a person may need

Figure 4.3   Function-Based Organization

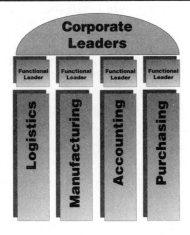

Figure 4.4   Pre-Workplace View of Menu Structure

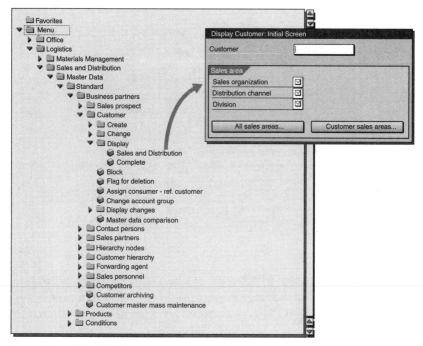

Source: Copyright by SAP AG.

to refer to data about the customer. But the sales-order creation resides in one area of the sales system while the customer record sits in a different area. The sales-order clerk has to move to two different parts of an extensive menu structure to locate the information required to finish creating the sales order. Figure 4.4 illustrates the traditional menu structure that is based on the system and its functions.

Process-Based Organizations

Representing an advance over function-based organizations, process-based organizations focus on the end-to-end core business processes necessary to meet customer needs and generate shareholder value. Figure 4.5 illustrates a simple process-based organization.

Figure 4.5   Process-Based Organization

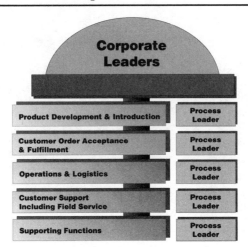

With the removal of functional silos comes a disbursement of responsibility and a shifting of accountability. In such a process organization, although process owners/leaders still exist, the organization of processes is no longer hierarchical. Multi-functional teams are responsible for process outcomes, and responsibility for fulfilling tasks that help meet the company's business objectives increases for individuals at all organizational levels.

In a process-focused business environment, companies base their competitive position on their core competencies. They outsource supporting activities and processes that are not key to their competitive position. They partner with companies that possess the competencies and processes they need to deliver the next generation of products to customers and value to shareholders, and they sell off competencies and processes they no longer require.

Globalization, geographic mobility, rapidly changing technology, and new business relationships (outsourcing, joint ventures, spin-offs) expand the scope of a process-oriented company's potential business models and of what the company can do to meet market needs and business objectives. But the IT systems employed in a process-based organization, even ERP systems, still do not fully provide appropriate tools for managing the process flow. Systems remain hierarchical and menus still show many applications that most users do not need. To move forward, more flexible systems are necessary to help assign tasks and responsibilities in a fluid way in order to redesign processes in real time when the need arises.

FROM FUNCTION- AND PROCESS-BASED TO ROLE-BASED

Today, many companies are moving to a roles-based focus, organizing tasks and activities not only by the processes to which they belong, but also by the roles that perform them. Figure 4.6 illustrates a role-based menu structure. In contrast to the menu structure illustrated in Figure 4.4, this menu structure allows the order-entry clerk to get to where he or she needs to be in two or three clicks.

A particular set of activities and tasks undertaken by one role might be part of many different processes. Today, roles are dynamic and reflect innovation and the changing nature of business. Traditional process reengineering cannot accommodate these changes; role updating can.

The current generation of corporate leaders understands that roles have, more than ever before, a real impact on how the company operates. Business results are similarly affected by the activities undertaken in multiple roles; top-level roles are no longer the only ones that drive business performance.

In a role-based organization, significantly more fluidity exists between roles and processes. Roles are increasingly responsible for initiating process change. Individuals who perform tasks within roles and who are accountable for tasks and activities within a process require IT systems that are integrated, particularly where processes are broken up and not visibly integrated. If parts of processes exist in different locations within systems, working individuals must be able at least to receive a visual, top-level integration, making navigating between the different elements of the process almost intuitive. The workplace makes this possible. The static portion of a process can often be performed by using the company's internal systems. But the dynamic portion often requires interaction with other people and access to information and applications found outside the company's enterprise resource planning (ERP) system.

Figure 4.6   Role-Based View of Menu Structure

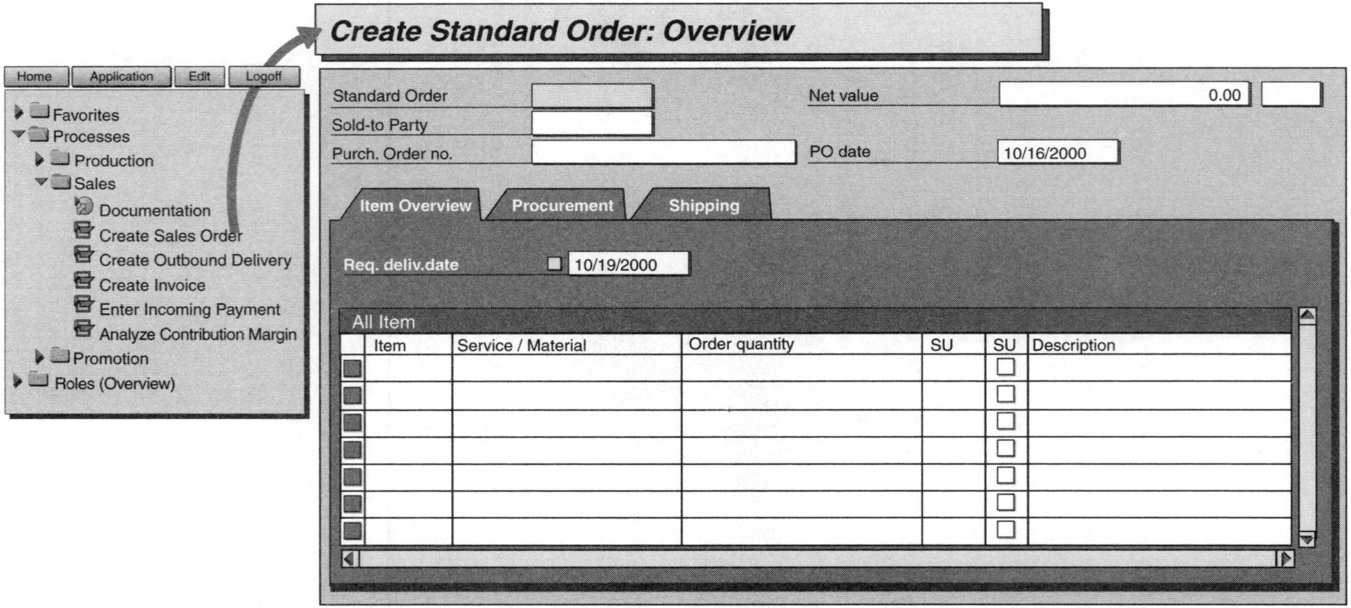

Source: Copyright by SAP AG.

Recognition that roles have a great impact on corporate operations has prompted a turnaround in the mechanisms used to expedite changes in the way people work. In a process-based organization, a change to either the processes or the systems is labor intensive. Such changes require an expert configuration team to carry out the implementation, and, potentially, retraining, depending on the degree of change involved. This is a top-down process; all change goes through various levels of approval and can be very time-consuming.

In a role-based organization, the prevalence of change at every level means that every role—and its associated workplace—must be flexible and dynamic enough to handle such change. To meet this need, change can be driven through a role. A role redesign can, in some cases, replace process reengineering as a rapid, dynamic method of change that occurs faster and requires less configuration expertise. Change in this environment is, therefore, much easier to implement and serves the individual much better than process reengineering.

Role Development

Generic solutions to business problems need to be adaptable. The same is true for generic roles. And the goal of a role-based IT architecture is flexibility and fluidity.

Companies that deliver workplace technology and design workplaces for businesses deliver pre-defined role templates. But these are merely starting points. The differences in industry, market, geography, and corporate culture require that role participants customize their roles to match more closely how they actually undertake tasks and activities in order to meet business objectives.

WHAT IMPLEMENTERS SHOULD KNOW

Importance of Role Definition

Because workplaces depend on roles, roles should be defined at an early stage. Role definitions drive the number or complexity of

MiniApps, system integration, drag and relate scenarios, and single sign-on requirements. Inherent in every role definition is the responsibility to integrate content from various internal and external sources; for example, company policies and procedures from the intranet, analysts reports from the Internet, currency conversion rates from a bank, and product information from a marketplace/exchange. Role definition, and, therefore, access security maintenance, must be carefully considered to ensure that the workplace not only meets the company's working, legal, and processing requirements, but also can be easily maintained after the new systems have been implemented.

Impact of Role Focus

Now, more than ever, companies must identify and create access requirements that, while generic, still meet the organization's objectives. The workplace is the working individual's unique view of the world. If each user requires unique access requirements, a company of a thousand or more users would have to create an equal number of different workplaces and identify and code the workplace requirements for each individual. In ERP-only implementations, this level of generic access is not that important. Highly generic access level solutions were used mainly for global rollouts where users occupying the same position in different subsidiaries were given the same access profiles.

Given this more generic level of access across the company, companies must focus attention on the interaction of access and other system/business process controls in order to mitigate any risks that could arise and that could leave the company in a vulnerable position.

Planning a Workplace Implementation

Practically speaking, adding a workplace requires a review of the way ERP systems have been implemented to date. Traditionally, access to system users has been regulated by security and security profiles. Within a workplace, however, the security profile (the workplace role) is the workplace's backbone and driver.

While the method for granting access to ERP back-end systems has not changed, the access provided by a role goes well beyond that of an ERP system. For example, roles must include Web links to non-ERP systems, corporate reporting packages, Web pages and MiniApps pertinent to the process steps performed by any given role.

The security element with respect to role access has increased in importance and raises a number of significant questions:

- In an organization consisting of more than one legal entity, how does the company ensure that staff cannot access or update information between different entities where this information is not accessed or updated directly via the ERP system?
- How does a company control the type of information viewed at the end of external Web links, and how does it prevent users from accessing sites that are prohibited by company policy?
- How does a company protect its assets? (One way, for example, could be through segregation of duties.)
- With the use of the same generic "data entry" workplace for individuals updating different legal entities, how does the company ensure that their MiniApps grant access only to information pertinent to their entity?
- What is the best fit between granting each user in the company an individualized workplace as opposed to a limited number of generic workplaces, and how will this choice impact the level of system security?
- How easily can a range of different systems of different ages be integrated into a workplace?
- What will single sign-on require in terms of new technology?
- If a company is doing business over the Web, what level of encryption must be in place?
- Will single point of access be company wide (i.e., will all systems be integrated into the workplace) or will it relate only to a number of key systems)?
- If roles use a number of systems—some of which will not be accessed via the workplace—what does this mean in

terms of training, employee acceptance, and perception of this technological change?

- How does a company go about identifying new roles and their workplace requirements while ensuring that they do not compromise system security policies?

This last question is difficult to answer and will depend on the circumstances surrounding the implementation. Listed below are the three most common implementation scenarios and the access issues that need to be resolved:

- *Scenario 1: Workplace and ERP Implementation with No Business Process Reengineering.* A system is being implemented simply to replace one or more other systems without a large scale reengineering of business processes. Job/organizational roles and their links to each job title will already exist within the company. They may not be documented as roles, but they can be identified via job descriptions and discussions with those persons occupying each job title. In this scenario, the difficult task of identifying "who should do what" is already accomplished. The remaining tasks are to identify the relevant functionality, systems, and supporting information required by each role.
- *Scenario 2: Workplace and ERP Implementation with Business Process Reengineering/Organizational Change.* In an organization going through a merger or restructuring, or one that is simply reorganizing processes, business processes will be redefined. Therefore, new organization roles to fit these processes must be identified and defined in terms of the new system and processes. Organizational role definition is dependent on the stabilization of new processes and is a difficult task to achieve in a short time. Once new organizational roles are defined and system functionality is mapped, identification of required systems and supporting information can begin.
- *Scenario 3: Workplace Only Implementation.* In this example, the workplace is perceived as another layer sitting on top of all existing systems, which become transparent to the

user. Job roles and titles do not change; the user is simply given one all-encompassing, user-friendly view of the organization. This view will reflect how individuals need to work and will support them and provide a more flexible way of allowing them to complete their process steps. However, systems relevant to each user, along with Web links and MiniApps, still need to be identified.

Scenarios 1 and 2 identify a need to change the way role access (and thus security) is traditionally implemented on ERP projects. Access is usually left until the end of a project and is then rushed through right before go-live. Given the complicated nature of ERP systems' security, problems often arise when the company switches over to the new system (not having the correct authorization to fulfill completely the process steps that have been allocated) or usually 6 to 12 months afterward, where segregation of duties arise or user and role maintenance becomes unwieldy.

Implementing new systems is always costly. However, when systems are implemented correctly, the benefits can be immense and continuous. Roles play a key part in determining the timing and allocation of resources for such an implementation. Until the number of generic roles has been agreed upon and identified, the integration requirements, MiniApp development, and drag and relate and single sign-on requirements cannot be accurately estimated. Each new role, therefore, acts as a multiplier to the timing and resource levels of the implementation. Therefore, it is important to approach a workplace implementation understanding the impact role numbers can have and to work toward a solution that accommodates not only the company and its ways of working, but also the implementation budget.

Ultimate Significance of Roles

Roles allow user focus to come to the fore. They, not technology, are the drivers for integrating different systems into the workplace. Identifying links to other sites (e.g., supplier catalogues accessed over the Internet) results from the interaction among companies facilitated by the Internet. However, even this level of integration is, in fact, integration of users and systems or users and users. In short, the hard distinctions between companies and systems are disappearing.

A role is more than just a job description. The workplace is a tool that empowers users while providing the company with more effective working individuals who are more satisfied with their jobs because they have more control over the way they work. With increased accountability at all levels of the company comes increased responsibility and a heightened sense of worth. Working individuals are, therefore, more willing to go the extra distance in performing their job activities/tasks well.

If the individual who will live in a role is involved in designing and building it, he or she will be much more likely to utilize to the fullest extent possible the role and the IT system behind it. Only the individual who will live the role has the fundamental understanding of what is required of his or her workplace, in terms of both practical material and comfort.

Previously, the implementation partner defined these IT system requirements. But now it is clear that up-front involvement by the individual who will live the role increases the chances that the system implementation will be successful. Giving individuals a stake in defining their roles and in designing the way those roles interface with the IT systems that support them minimizes the potential for user backlash that might result in a costly system rebuilding effort.

5

A Day in the Life of a Workplace: Three Roles

Each working day, individuals throughout a company use the workplace to complete the tasks necessary to perform their jobs. Within the workplace, each individual has a number of *roles*. In each role, he or she participates in a number of *business scenarios*. In turn, these business scenarios are implemented using *components* of the workplace software. Figure 5.1 illustrates these elements as they would apply to a purchasing transaction and highlights the particular role being played in the scenario.

In this chapter, we will look at how three people use the workplace: the company's chief financial officer (CFO), a sales manager, and a field service engineer. We begin by describing the roles of each of these individuals and then demonstrate how they use the workplace during the course of a day.

ROLES: CFO

In the 1950s, the role of a CFO was clearly defined and predictable. He (in the 1950s, just about every CFO was a he) was the "corporate policeman," in charge of instituting and maintaining financial controls, allocating resources across various product lines, structuring financial arrangements, and producing financial reports. His work, and the work of his staff, was transaction and detail oriented and tedious. He was responsible for reconciling

69

Figure 5.1 People Filling Roles Perform Tasks within Scenarios, Supported by Technical Components

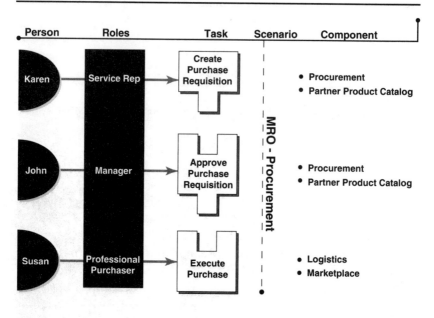

thousands of requisitions, purchase orders, invoices, and receipts. The reports he issued were all backward looking, focusing on how money had been spent.

Today's CFO is far more focused on value creation. He or she utilizes both internal and external information to support decision-making and guide the enterprise. According to a 1997 study by the Conference Board, a U.S. research organization, CFOs spend up to 50 percent of each day focusing on corporate strategy and on potential mergers, acquisitions, and other strategic alliances. They spend the other 50 percent on traditional accounting and control issues, as well as on external reporting to shareholders and regulatory authorities, so-called fiduciary responsibilities. A 1992 Coopers & Lybrand study of CFOs found that most were still spending 75 to 80 percent of their time on these responsibilities. Reporting similar results in 1993, *CFO* magazine stated that financial staff were spending 66 percent of their time on transactions, 18 percent on controls, 11 percent on decision support, and 5 percent on management.

The 1997 Conference Board study also correlated time spent on strategic issues with company share price and found that in terms of stock price, companies whose CFOs spent more than 20 percent of their time on strategy/strategic alliance issues were more likely to outperform competitors. As illustrated in Figure 5.2, the role of the CFO continues to change. These changes and

Figure 5.2   Role of the CFO Continues To Evolve

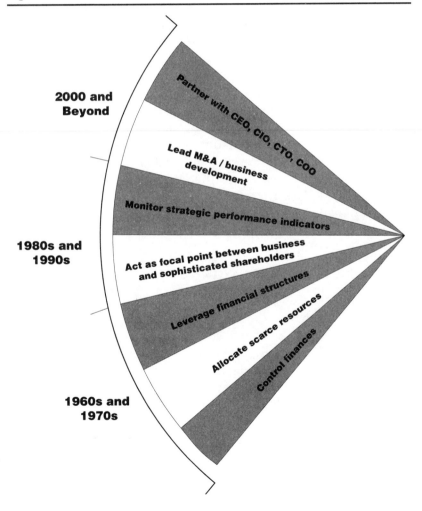

new functions enable CFOs to respond more rapidly to changes in business conditions. The workplace for today's CFO, therefore, must support both day-to-day business reporting responsibilities as well as long-term strategic tasks.

ROLES: SALES MANAGER

Years ago, the sales manager's job was to report results from the sales force to the vice president of sales or business unit president, who made all of the strategic sales-related decisions. Today, in most companies, the sales manager's responsibilities have become far more strategic. Where this is the case, it is the result of decision-making having been pushed down closer to the customer.

Today's sales manager is in charge of planning, organizing, and implementing sales strategy for a country or region within a country or for a product or product line; defining and striving to attain overall sales objectives and sales profitability for a geographic or product unit; overseeing the sales force and/or distributor network; and coordinating budgets, forecasts, and reports on products and pricing trends. Figure 5.3 illustrates the evolution of the sales manager role over the last 30 to 40 years. The sales manager's workplace, therefore, must allow him or her to monitor the sales pipeline, sales portfolio, and sales budget, as well as his or her sales activities and those of all the sales reps in the group.

ROLES: FIELD SERVICE ENGINEER

Like the roles of CFO and sales manager, the field service engineer's role has changed over time. This change is due to the increasing complexity of much of the technology he or she must service and to the increased prominence of the role as it applies to customer relationship management.

A generation ago, the field service engineer arrived at the shop in the morning, checked a list of repair stops, pulled the job tickets for that day's work, selected the tools and parts necessary to make those repairs, and proceeded on his route. He recorded the stops he made, the tasks he performed, and the repairs he was unable to perform because he lacked the parts or the proper tools. A supervisor sorted out this information at the end of the day. The

Figure 5.3   Role of the Sales Manager Continues To Evolve

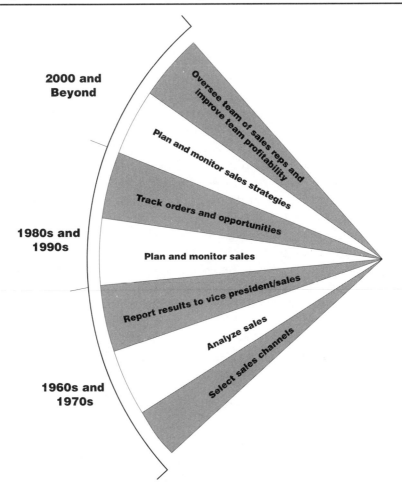

2000 and Beyond

Oversee team of sales reps and improve team profitability

Plan and monitor sales strategies

Track orders and opportunities

1980s and 1990s

Plan and monitor sales

Report results to vice president/sales

Analyze sales

Select sales channels

1960s and 1970s

next day the field service engineer would go out again, but this time, the supervisor would try to ensure that he had the right tools and parts to complete repairs from the previous day.

By the 1980s, the creation of job tickets had been automated and many of the necessary parts were shipped directly to the site. The field service engineer, therefore, did not physically have to pick up the parts each morning. He or she was increasingly responsible for the maintenance component that kept the installed base running, as well as for performing repairs as needed. In addition, the field service engineer was responsible for keeping track of time and expenses for client billing purposes.

Today, the field service engineer's tasks and responsibilities continue to grow. In addition to performing service activities at customer sites and providing feedback about completed tasks, the field service engineer, as part of the customer service team, must also analyze and maintain customer, warranty, and contractual information. In addition, he or she has responsibility for maintaining the spare-parts inventory, planning spare-parts demand, and performing available-to-promise checks on parts; and for coordinating service requests and service orders with other members of the field service team. If he or she is unable to perform a service request, the field service engineer is responsible for transferring that request to another team member's calendar.

Figure 5.4 illustrates the evolution of the field service engineer role over the last 30 to 40 years. The field service engineer's workplace must provide him or her access to customer information regarding the installed base, as well as to information about parts inventories and preventive maintenance schedules. It must also enable the field service engineer to alert others about common failures he or she has noted.

CFO'S DAY

CFO Roberta Jones arrives at her office early. Today, she and her staff will close the books for the company's fiscal third quarter. When this task was performed manually, it could take weeks to complete. However, with the help of the enterprise resource planning (ERP) system the company installed in the mid-1990s and with the consolidation over the past few years of many accounting functions into a global shared service center, the closing is no more than a two-day chore. But they are long days. Although she and her core staff have the process well choreographed, getting the job done right is still a difficult task.

Jones would have preferred to delay this task for a few weeks. The third quarter closing was deflecting her attention from an important strategic matter. She had almost completed the due dili-

Figure 5.4   Role of the Field Service Engineer Continues To Evolve

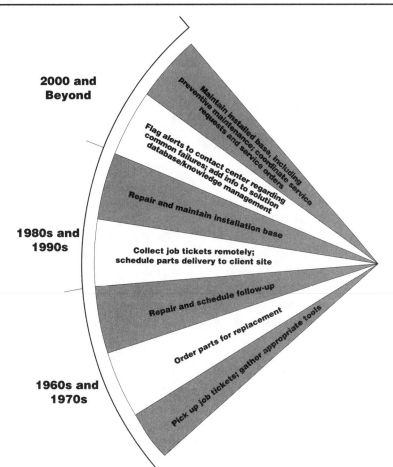

2000 and Beyond

Maintain installed base, including preventive maintenance; coordinate service requests and service orders

Flag alerts to contact center regarding common failures; add info to solution database/knowledge management

Repair and maintain installation base

1980s and 1990s

Collect job tickets remotely; schedule parts delivery to client site

Repair and schedule follow-up

Order parts for replacement

1960s and 1970s

Pick up job tickets; gather appropriate tools

gence effort begun three weeks ago involving a company the CEO would like to acquire. He has been negotiating this deal with the other company's CEO for a little more than a month, and, before competitors get wind of it, was hoping to settle on a price.

Not so long ago, a merger or acquisition would have taken months to negotiate and investigate, and companies could keep their talks quiet for that long. But today, with analysts and financial journalists practically hiding in the walls of corporate headquarters, even a complicated transaction like a merger must be conducted very rapidly. The workplace allows the CFO to juggle these multiple responsibilities. By pushing much of the necessary data, the workplace eliminates the need for the CFO to find important information through searches or menus.

CFO Using Her Workplace

Figure 5.5 is the opening screen Jones sees when she enters her company's workplace. The screen contains a consolidation monitor that allows her to supervise the financial consolidation for the third quarter closing. She needs both a good overview of the process to set up consolidated financial statements and information about the progress of the related closing. The screen also contains a data monitor that allows her to see the progress of the various tasks her staff is performing.

The data monitor and the consolidation monitor are her control panels. Using them, she can drill down to detailed information. Strategic enterprise management (SEM) business consolidation supports legal accounting rules as well as management reporting by user-defined reporting units.

Using the data monitor by task, Jones can monitor the consolidation process itself. The SEM business information collection functionality pushes market and competitor information that has been gathered at any given moment from various sources (such as Internet and proprietary information providers) directly to the CFO's desk. If any balance differences exist, the financial team needs to react and send out e-mails to various organizational units to reconcile them.

In Figure 5.6, Jones uses the balanced scorecard within the workplace not only as a planning and performance-monitoring tool, but also for communication. The balanced scorecard displays an overview of the individual's objectives and their status from four different perspectives: financial, internal, learning, and growth. She can use this monitor to drill down to the individual measures and their current status.

Since she does a lot of due diligence work in her company's constant search for acquisitions and joint-venture partners, she has also set filings from the U.S. Securities and Exchange Com-

Figure 5.5 CFO's Workplace

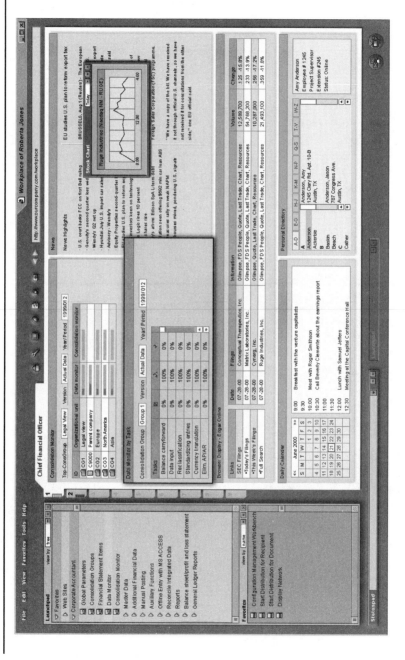

Figure 5.6 CFO Uses Balanced Scorecard

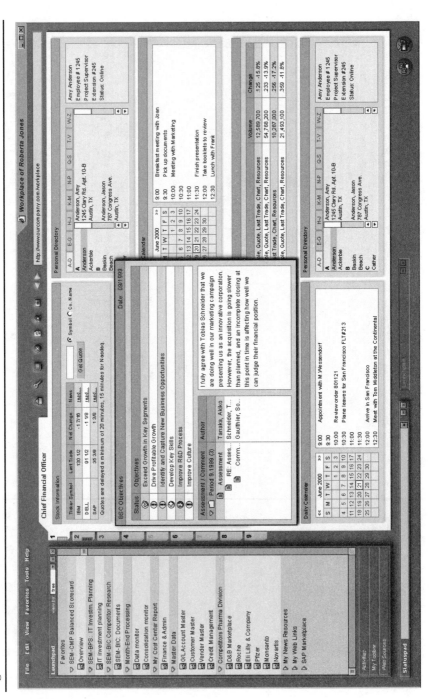

mission (SEC) as one of her news resources. The system she uses provides a wealth of information about both routine and special filings made by companies and their executives to the SEC under Unites States securities law. Looking at the SEC filings page, she develops a number of questions, and decides that she should speak with the corporate controller for the target company. Figure 5.7 illustrates the workplace's ability to overlay a video-conference call on to the SEC filings page.

While the CFO is meeting with her staff to assign the day's tasks for the quarterly financial closing at headquarters, half a world away in Frankfurt, Germany, a sales manager, Peter Maier, is ending his own long day.

SALES MANAGER'S DAY

Maier has decided to start a three-month campaign to sell an add-on product to current customers. He must determine the overall schedule and budget for the campaign, put together a sales team and choose a leader, create a telemarketing campaign, determine which customers to target, and initiate and monitor the development prototypes and sales collateral materials.

Throughout the three-month campaign, he closely monitors sales, revenue, and expenses. He needs historical data about the past day, week, and month. This data helps him determine how to deploy resources during the next few days and weeks. He needs to know how much has been spent on the sales campaign and how much revenue the effort has generated, which members of his sales staff are producing sales and which are not, which customers have been contacted, and which category of customers are purchasing what volume of product.

Sales Manager Using His Workplace

Figure 5.8 illustrates graphically and numerically how the campaign is progressing. A bar chart showing both sales and cost of sales overlays a calendar, a message board from the sales staff, and other data. Maier selects the bar chart that highlights the cost of sales for the previous four weeks to make a determination about how to move his sales campaign forward.

Figure 5.7 CFO Has a Video Conference

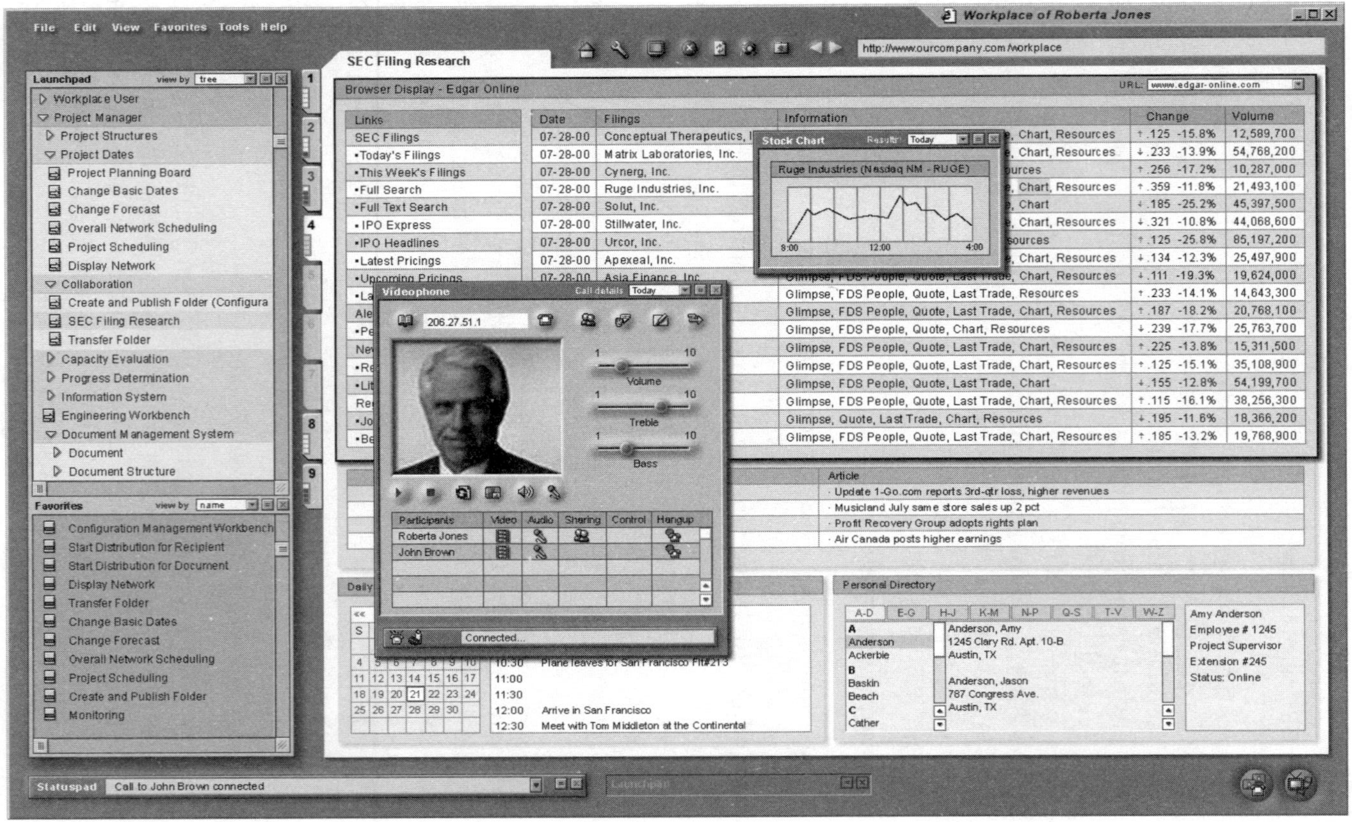

Figure 5.8   Sales Manager's Workplace

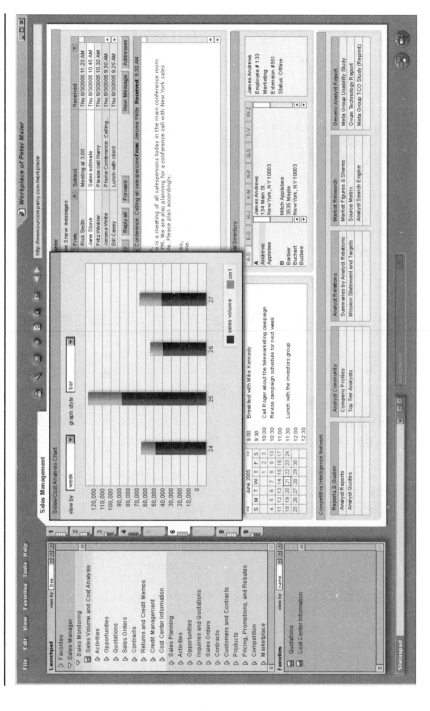

Figure 5.9 illustrates another view of important data for the sales manager. Here he chooses to highlight the chart, which enables him to analyze the value and share of the sales revenue being generated by each member of the sales team and the share of the costs of sales for which each member is accountable. He discovers that four sales people are generating more revenue than costs, while for one, costs are exceeding revenue.

In Figure 5.10 Maier drills down to sales revenue by customer for the most recent week of the campaign.

Finally, in Figure 5.11, Maier analyzes the opportunity pipeline for the next five weeks of the campaign. Noting a two-week period showing little activity in any phase of the sales decision cycle, Maier can focus his team's energy on generating activity in that time frame.

FIELD SERVICE ENGINEER'S DAY

While Jones in Austin, Texas, and Maier in Frankfurt are dealing with their strategic issues, Ana Gonzalez, the field service engineer in Buenos Aires, is also trying to solve a problem. On each of the past three days, she has visited a customer site and encountered the same problem with the same unit. Today's next call is to another customer with the same unit, and the problem—as described in a note from the technical support person who spoke with the customer—sounds very similar to those she encountered during the past few days.

Before she drives to the customer site, Gonzalez checks to make sure that she has the necessary tools and parts and finds that she does. But she is troubled by a nagging thought. Last year during a six-month period, she had done quite a bit of post-installation work adjusting these units in at least two dozen sites around the city.

If this is a part that is going to start failing at all of those customers' sites, she needs to be sure that enough spare parts are in the pipeline. Gonzalez wants to collect some information from customers about machine utilization and determine if the need for replacements correlates with the design engineers' forecasts. A customer service alert might be necessary. And finally, she knows from scanning the field tech communications that this unit is pop-

Figure 5.9 Sales Manager Reviews Salesperson Performance

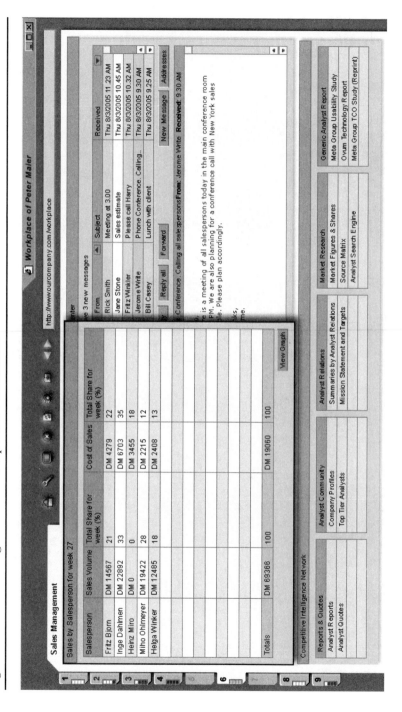

Figure 5.10   Sales by Customer

Workplace of Peter Maier

http://www.ourcompany.com/workplace

Sales Management

Sales by Customer for week 27

Customer	Sales Volume	CM1	DB1%
Elektromarkt Bamby	DM 4445.85	DM 3067.10	69.0
Lampen-Market GmbH	DM 3021.31	DM 1595.45	52.8
Institut fuer Umweltforschung	DM 9748.50	DM 7494.40	76.9
Hitech AG	DM 6750.90	DM 6750.90	100
Chirstal Clear	DM 1384.81	DM 544.49	39.3
Bay Cable Advertising	DM 6367.40	DM 5054.10	79.3
Karlsson High Tech Markt	DM 12763.60	DM 3796.70	29.7
Motormarkt Heidelberg GmbH	DM 8260.40	DM 3732.90	45.2
Grensen AG	DM 5543.17	DM 2305.88	41.6
Enevold Technik	DM 11071.00	DM 3354.16	30.3

View Graph

Competitive Intelligence Network

Reports & Quotes	Analyst C ommunity	Analyst Relations	Market Research
Analyst Reports	Company Profiles	Summaries by Analyst Relations	Market Figures & Shares
Analyst Quotes	Top Tier Analysts	Mission Statement and Targets	Source Matrix
			Analyst Search Engine

Generic Analyst Report
Meta Group Usability Study
Ovum Technology Report
Meta Group TCO Study (Reprint)

ve 3 new messages

From	Subject	Received
Rick Smith	Meeting at 3.00	Thu 8/3/2005 11.23 AM
Jane Stone	Sales estimate	Thu 8/3/2005 10.45 AM
Fritz Winkler	Please call Harry	Thu 8/3/2005 10.32 AM
Jerome Write	Phone Conference. Calling.	Thu 8/3/2005 9.30 AM
Bill Casey	Lunch with client	Thu 8/3/2005 9.25 AM

Reply all   Forward   New Message   Addresses

e Conference. Calling all salespersons **From:** Jerome Write **Received:** 9.30 AM

e is a meeting of all salespersons today in the main conference room
PM. We are also planning for a conference call with New York sales
le. Please plan accordingly.

ks,
me.

84

Figure 5.11   Opportunity Pipeline

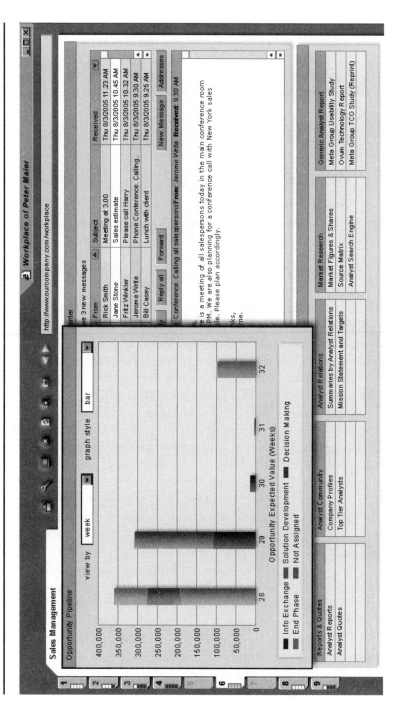

ular throughout South America and has been installed at literally hundreds of sites.

Field Service Engineer Using Her Workplace

As a field service engineer, Gonzalez does not always have access to a workplace on a desktop PC. But with the increasing availability of mobile devices, she can still access a considerable amount of content, including troubleshooting logs, reports, work orders, and customer service records. Such devices allow Gonzalez and her colleagues to be more responsive to customer needs than ever before. Mobile devices dynamically link the dispatcher and the field services engineer. In this way, Gonzalez can change her schedule as needed to better meet customer priorities.

Such devices do not merely capture data. They enable Gonzalez to, in effect, take her whole system with her. While content is important, mobile devices also increase the availability of the field service engineer. More than just messaging or telephone systems, they enable the field service engineer to perform applications without being tied to a physical location or workstation.

Figure 5.12 illustrates a mobile communication device, with information for Gonzalez about a repair problem.

After making the repair, Gonzalez logs in the time she spent on the job, as well as any materials and parts she used (Figure 5.13). She can immediately send this information to field service management for her productivity reporting and also to invoicing personnel for appropriate and speedy customer billing. Charging time and expenses immediately after each job improves Gonzalez's productivity because she no longer has to take time at the end of the day to reconstruct her activities and enter all of her billing data.

Increasingly, cell phones are being designed for Web access. Figure 5.14 illustrates a mobile phone with the ability to display a service order list. Gonzalez has been asked to field test a new line of mobile phones. Although she likes the ease of use and portability of the phone, there is one disadvantage. The screen on the phone is especially small and cannot hold much information at one time.

Figure 5.12   FSE's Mobile Workplace

Figure 5.13   Entering Time Information

Figure 5.14   WAP Workplace

While mobile devices can increase productivity on the road, they are not yet as easy to use as the computer-based workplace. Therefore, when Gonzalez can get to her laptop, she uses her workplace to access information about billing and shipping for future maintenance and repairs (Figure 5.15) and to obtain a complete list of the next day's service orders (Figure 5.16).

The workplace allows Gonzalez to overlay on the general screen the aspect she wishes to view. Using this workplace feature, she is able to move quickly and easily among these discrete information sections without having to close one window in order to open another.

Figure 5.15   FSE'S Desktop Workplace

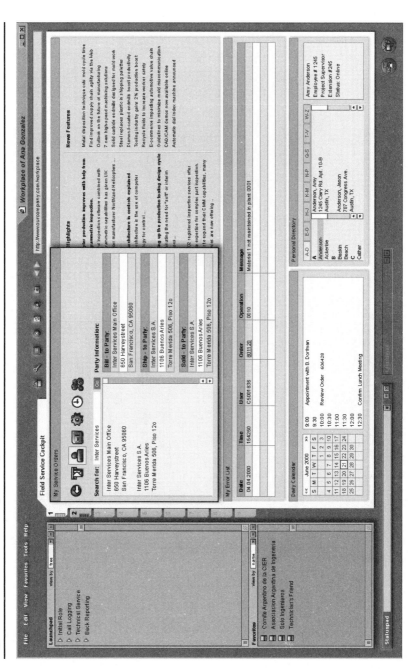

Figure 5.16   Reviewing Work Order Information

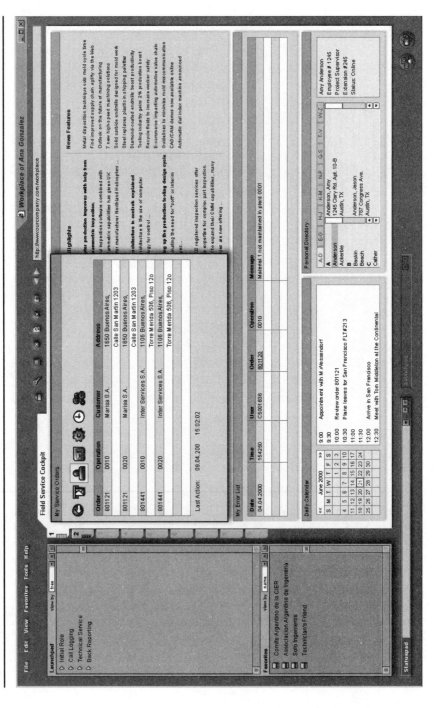

6

Communities and Marketplaces

A company can extend the value of its workplace by involving its customers, suppliers, and business partners in a virtual community. Such communities might even take the form of a marketplace, a business hub on the Internet where companies use existing channels to buy, sell, or trade goods, services, and information with their current business partners and/or to establish new channels for existing and new customers or suppliers.

Using workplace technology, an individual can seamlessly enter virtual communities and marketplaces, some operated and managed by the company and others by third parties or by a new organization or company that the community/marketplace founders create. We make the following distinction between a broadly defined community and a marketplace, which is in fact one type of community: A company can create a *community* based on an external community portal in order to manage relationships. That company uses a *marketplace* to execute transactions.

By creating a community that includes its suppliers, customers, and other collaborators , a company with a strong workplace can add value to its partner organizations. It does this by providing the working individuals within those organizations either with content, convenience, or both. Using the workplace, community members can access industry-specific products and services, as well as such specific content as industry reports covering analysis, trends, and events, and such general content as news, sports, weather, and stocks. They can also access chat rooms and hosted forums related to their roles.

Through its external community portal, a company can allow individuals within its partner companies to participate in some of the services that its own employees use. For example, if employees of the workplace-sponsoring company make their personal as well as business travel plans through a preferred provider of travel services, these services could be provided through the external community portal. In this way, employees at partner organizations could reap the same discounts as the workplace host's employees, and the workplace host could even negotiate deeper discounts based on the larger volume of business it generates for the travel service provider.

STRUCTURAL ISSUES INVOLVED IN DEVELOPING A COMMUNITY

Any company wishing to extend use of its workplace to a wider external community needs to answer three questions about how it will organize the community:

1. Will the community be content focused or merely provide convenience in the existing environment?
2. Will the community be available for on-demand use, with no fixed meetings or timelines for deliverables, or will it be more structured?
3. Will the community be innovative, expanding to meet more and more needs of community members, or will it concentrate on a fixed set of business issues, such as sales and procurement?

A company can structure its external community portal in one of three ways:

1. As an open community
2. As a syndicator
3. As a member-based community.

Open communities focus on providing information and building brand image on the site. The community Web site links to many other Web sites. Open communities receive most of their revenues by selling advertising to those who wish to reach individuals who, by logging on, have declared themselves to be a part of the community. Examples of open communities are ZDNet and Yahoo!.

Syndicators resell, repackage, and distribute products provided by others. Like open communities, syndicators focus on building their own brand image rather than those of the products they distribute. Syndicators derive most of their revenue from commissions resulting from the provision of distribution services. Examples of syndicators are Amazon.com and eBay.

Member-based communities can use marketplaces to execute transactions and optimize processes. If such a community succeeds, the community site will not require a brand. Any company wishing to do business with one of the companies that control the community will be forced to use it. Revenue for the managers of member-based sites is contractual, and in some instances sellers pay a commission and in others buyers pay a membership fee.

Any workplace-enabled company interested in hosting a community or marketplace can begin small by developing an external community portal just for the benefit of its suppliers, customers, and other business partners. Such an external-community portal features secure access for all collaborators, zero installation of applications, and pre-defined roles (Figure 6.1).

The increasing use of mobile devices, such as cell phones, two-way pagers, and personal digital assistants (PDA), means that such a community portal is accessible at any time from any place.

Who Drives the Community's Formation?

Suppliers or customers within an industry or an independent third party looking to create a meeting place for sellers and buyers within an industry can drive the formation of a content-based community or a transaction-based marketplace. Figure 6.2 highlights some of the organizations that have successfully created external communities or marketplaces.

Figure 6.1   External Community Portal

Figure 6.2   Types of Communities and Marketplaces

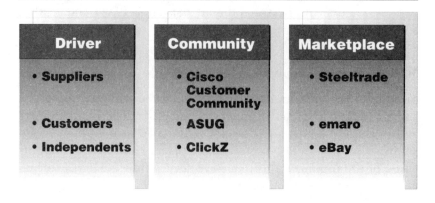

For example, on the supplier side, Cisco has created a very effective external community for its switching equipment customers, a content-rich site for those responsible for the installation and technical up-keep of its equipment. In the marketplace space, Steeltrade.com is a consortium of steel makers who are trying to move buyers of steel—from car makers to bridge-construction companies—to place their specifications on the Steeltrade site and solicit bids from marketplace members.

From the customer perspective, the Americas SAP User Group (ASUG) is a community of SAP software users who came together to exchange ideas, implementation techniques, and lessons learned, and to create and submit to SAP AG development requests based upon the functionality requirements of member groups. Emaro is a business procurement marketplace driven by Deutsche Bank and SAP.

In the independent space, ClickZ is an example of a content-rich community for marketing professionals. It focuses its offerings on e-marketing information. eBay is one of many examples of independent marketplaces. An interesting hybrid is WebMD, which provides health-related content to a lay audience and specialized offerings to physicians (e.g., medical insurance claims processing, Web-based pharmaceuticals purchasing, and medical supplies).

WHAT IS A MARKETPLACE?

The workplace provides the working individual with intuitive access to marketplaces through which transactions are conducted and processes are enhanced. A marketplace optimizes a network of businesses, rather than a single business, as illustrated in Figure 6.3. Marketplaces are created by consortiums of participants to enable them to conduct business activities—direct and indirect materials purchasing, for example—over the Web to, for instance, share in volume purchase discounts. To form the marketplace, each founding participant invests capital in the form of resources, actual funding, or services to be provided and receives stock in return. Subsequent marketplace members may buy stock and/or pay transaction fees to participate.

Figure 6.3   What Is an E-Market?

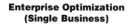

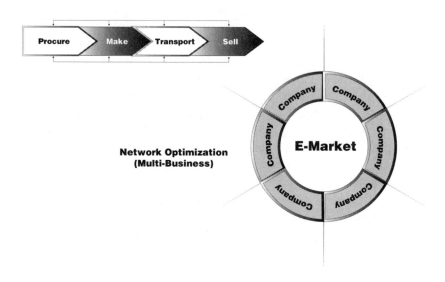

Virtual marketplaces are very much like their terrestrial counterparts. For example, Wakefern, a non-virtual marketplace-type organization based in the United States, was created by the owners of ShopRite supermarkets to procure, warehouse, and distribute groceries and merchandise to their independently owned stores. This arrangement gives the individual owners the buying power they need to compete with other large U.S. supermarket chains. Virtual marketplaces are forming for similar reasons with this difference: Because of the Internet's global reach, the stakes and competitive challenges are much higher and the potential benefits much greater.

Today, new marketplaces are forming rapidly. As Figure 6.4 illustrates, competing marketplaces are already in heated races for market share. Success is determined not only by which is first to market, but also by which is first to scale and by which attracts the critical mass of important players in its industry.

Figure 6.4   Importance of Speed to Market and Scale

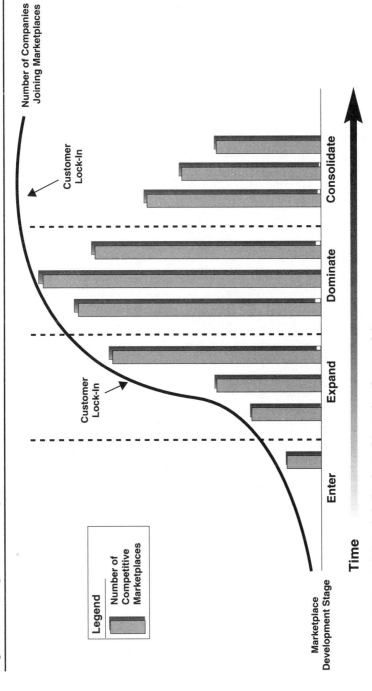

Sources: Forrester Research, Goldman Sachs, Bear Stearns, PricewaterhouseCoopers analysis.

Vertical and Horizontal Marketplaces

Whether formed around vertical or horizontal communities, marketplaces are based on a clear value proposition. Vertical-community marketplaces resolve industry-specific supply-chain inefficiencies, while horizontal-community marketplaces cut across industries and automate functional processes such as logistics or the purchase of maintenance, repair, and operations (MRO) materials. However they are structured, marketplaces provide a central platform for transaction automation, demand aggregation, improved market liquidity, and extended market reach.

A vertical marketplace is one in which transactions occur among some industry players from any portion of that industry's value chain. A horizontal marketplace addresses a particular function or group of functions across many industries. For example, a marketplace for procurement of non-production goods such as office supplies for purchasers in any industry is a horizontal marketplace. So is a human resources marketplace, which lists training opportunities, providers of benefit management services, and so on, for human resource professionals in any industry.

Integration Is Key

With marketplace technology that is integrated with both the seller's and the buyer's systems, participants can record multiple transactions with only one action. For example, when an employee makes an authorized purchase in the marketplace by clicking on the Web page "order" button, a number of different transactions are recorded, even though, from the user's perspective, only one transaction has actually taken place:

- The company's purchasing system will record that a purchase has taken place and may even signal for a payment to be made.
- The marketplace's software signals that it has been involved in a purchase and that it should collect a commission from the seller.

- The seller's systems will record an order through the particular marketplace and, depending on the relationship with the marketplace, may also record the buyer's identity.

However, as of May 2000, AMR Research estimated that only 20 of more than 600 existing marketplaces provided customers with such integration options. The next generation of marketplaces, AMR and others argue, will have to offer integration if they are to succeed.

MARKETPLACE MEMBER OR MARKETPLACE MAKER

How can a company best benefit from a marketplace opportunity? There are benefits both to using a marketplace as a member and to being a marketplace maker, that is, one of the founding partners.

The benefits of marketplace membership depend on whether the company is a buyer or a seller. For buyers, the primary benefits are reduction of procurement costs, more efficient logistics, and broader exposure to suppliers. For sellers, the primary benefits are reduction of cost of sales, access to broader markets, and improved ability to manage customer relationships. However, marketplaces are rapidly evolving beyond the simple buyer-seller model to a tightly integrated supply-chain management model, enabling such benefits as collaborative planning, forecasting, catalog management, and document exchange.

The benefits of being a marketplace maker include potential return on equity, potentially significant market valuation for the company's share in the marketplace, influence over design and construction of the marketplace, and market perception as an e-business leader. Clearly, the benefits of being a marketplace maker are greater than those of being a marketplace member, but so are the risks.

Finding the right partners is the key to founding a successful new marketplace. Five key partners or groups of partners are necessary:

1. An entrepreneurial management team, usually drawn from the marketplace making organizations

2. A software and technology partner
3. A marketplace builder and integration partner
4. An operational support partner to provide back-office software and hardware processing
5. A group of anchor buyers and sellers.

Marketplace success depends on five critical success factors:

1. *Deep industry knowledge.* The partners must be able to leverage industry-specific and cross-industry best practices from other marketplaces.
2. *Open participation.* The marketplace must not be skewed to the needs of any one participant.
3. *Business excellence.* Marketplace makers must understand how to create and operate a new entity.
4. *Numerous offerings.* The marketplace needs to offer several products and services in order to bring value to its members. These include direct and indirect procurement, content management, logistics, and collaborative planning.
5. *A clear value proposition.* Cost removed from the system must be quantifiable and sustainable if participants are to remain with the marketplace, thus generating revenue to the marketplace makers.

Strategy in a World of Marketplaces

Companies all along the value chains in every industry—from raw-materials suppliers to finished-goods manufacturers—need to formulate strategies not only to survive but to prosper in a world in which new business models are being created on a weekly, and sometimes daily, basis. In this current business climate, corporate leadership is uncertain of the technology involved in becoming an e-company and of what kind of business model to adopt once they have transformed themselves from "bricks and mortar" to "clicks and mortar" enterprises.

From small regional companies to global giants, CEOs are asking the same questions:

- Should my company create a Web site that fosters a strong brand and try to sell from there?
- Should we participate in a marketplace and sell that way?
- Should we do both?
- If we are going to participate in a marketplace, should it be one, a few, or many?
- Should we take an equity stake in a marketplace, or even try to create a marketplace based on our own relationships and external community portal?

Clearly, participation in marketplaces is not an option; it is a necessity. But future participants must understand that marketplaces do not just define how a company does business; they are new businesses in and of themselves. Procurement for example, is an essential component of marketplaces, but participation in an e-procurement effort will not, in and of itself, provide a company with competitive advantage.

MARKETPLACE GUIDING PRINCIPLES

Companies thinking about participating in a marketplace are faced with a myriad of tasks that need to be prioritized. The following principles may help such companies cut through the clutter and identify critical success factors:

- Leverage outsourcing for data center services and back-office applications.
- Minimize integration costs for e-market customers.
- Engineer for breakaway performance.
- Stress security and reliability.
- Attain balance between "best of breed" and "single source" for components.
- Insure "plug and play" compatibility in hardware and software.
- Business requirements drive technology, not vice-versa.
- Buy components. Build only when absolutely necessary.
- Make enrollment for customers a "non-event."

- Deliver seamless service; make linkage between components transparent.
- Develop self-sufficiency to maintain and grow critical business applications.
- Remember the customer at all times!

**TRANSORA MARKETPLACE ENABLES
GLOBAL B2B EFFICIENCIES**

More than 50 of the world's largest food, beverage, and consumer product manufacturers have created Transora, an electronic B2B marketplace. The largest collaborative effort in this industry's history, Transora will use the Internet to create global efficiencies. Participants include such "marquee" companies as Bristol-Myers Squibb, Cadbury Schweppes, Coca-Cola, Colgate-Palmolive, Diageo, Earthgrains, Embotelladora Andina, Fort James, General Mills, Gillette, Heineken, Heinz, Hershey Foods, Johnson & Johnson, Kellogg, Kraft, Nabisco, Nestlé, Orkla, Parmalat, PepsiCo, Procter & Gamble, Reckitt Benckiser, Sara Lee, and Unilever.

Transora will bring multiple buyers and sellers into a virtual marketplace providing service offerings in the following areas:

- **Procurement:** Procurement offerings enable Transora participants to purchase goods through catalogs or auctions, evaluate and certify vendors, and establish long-term strategic sourcing relationships.
- **Supply Chain:** Transora will provide the platform and capability for participants to integrate seamlessly and synchronize the value chain in order to deliver improved customer service via operational efficiency and effectiveness within and across enterprises.

- **Retail:** Retail service offerings will provide new platforms for the manufacturer/retailer relationship that will reduce transaction costs, improve market liquidity, and provide new, collaborative services resulting in enhanced levels of performance improvement and levels of consumer focus.

- **Content, Community, and Communication:** Transora will provide continuous industry and marketplace information and knowledge management tools to participants. In addition, Transora will ensure complete user-enabled functionality of each service offering.

Transora is also piloting connections with other exchanges.

Transora will leverage old-economy assets to create an effective new-economy business and will offer a universal solution that reduces costs and lowers risk for individual members. Ultimately, it will bring together buyers and sellers across the entire CPG value chain, improving the operational efficiency of their key processes.

7

A Day in the Life of Community Workplaces

Inside the enterprise, individuals utilize the workplace to perform the tasks necessary to do their jobs. But the true power of the workplace lies in its capacity to be used by those external to the enterprise. The workplace allows those within an enterprise to interact with all members of the enterprise ecosystem. This ecosystem is a web of relationships among suppliers of materials, components, and sub-assemblies; partners who provide information, applications, and services; customers; and end-users, all working as if they were part of one enterprise—a virtual enterprise. Each member of this web utilizes his or her workplace to enter the ecosystem's world of information, applications, and services, including marketplaces. The workplace becomes a virtual extension of an individual's network, where introductions can be made and deals can be negotiated—almost like being on a golf course.

While a consumer community workplace—what is traditionally known as a portal—is a collection of services oriented toward a community of consumers, an enterprise portal creates an enterprise-specific collaborative community. Such a community, established by one specific enterprise for its customers and suppliers, enables true collaboration and merging of business processes across enterprises.

An important distinction exists between the consumer community workplace and the enterprise community workplace that involves specific customers, business partners, and consumers. In this chapter, we will discuss only enterprise community workplaces. We will use collaborative planning and product design as examples to illustrate how an enterprise community workplace can provide seamless access to demand, forecast, engineering and design, and production scheduling information.

ENTERPRISE COMMUNITY WORKPLACE

The enterprise community workplace facilitates better collaboration among business partners by reducing organizational and technical boundaries and overall cost.

Reducing Organizational Boundaries

The enterprise community workplace tears down walls and enhances the exchange of information between companies. The result? The right person gets the right information at the right time.

Within the workplace, information can be managed tightly or loosely, depending on how much control the information "owner" wishes to impose, and how much he or she desires to cooperate or collaborate with other information providers and users.

Figure 7.1 illustrates simple one-to-one communication: A dialog occurs between the information owner and one other participant. The owner maintains control of the information.

Figure 7.1   Binary Communication

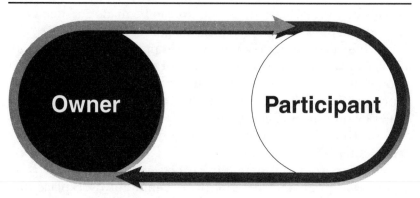

Figure 7.2   Communication with Internal Review

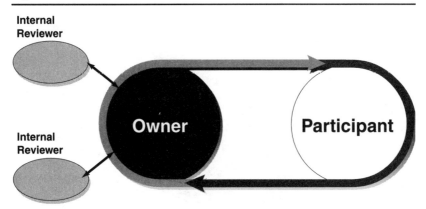

Figure 7.2 illustrates one-to-one communication with collaborative input from inside the enterprise. The information owner and process participant maintain the information loop, but the information owner also releases the information and collates responses from reviewers inside the enterprise.

Figure 7.3 illustrates one-to-many communication in a competitive mode (e.g., issuing a request for proposals and having each bidder respond). The information owner shares information with two process participants; each uses the information independently and responds independently to the information owner.

Figure 7.4 illustrates many-to-many communication in a fully collaborative mode. The information owner and the two information participants share information among themselves.

Reducing Technological Boundaries

Participating in an enterprise community workplace reduces or eliminates a company's need to use multiple technologies to accomplish intra-company communication. This is especially

Figure 7.3   One-to-Many (Competitive Case)

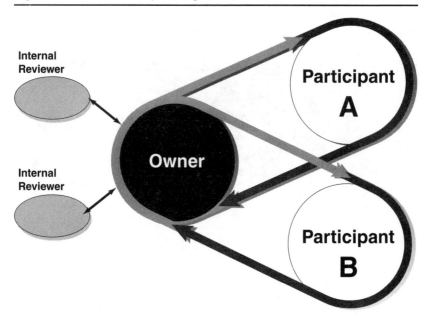

Figure 7.4   Many-to-Many (Collaborative Case)

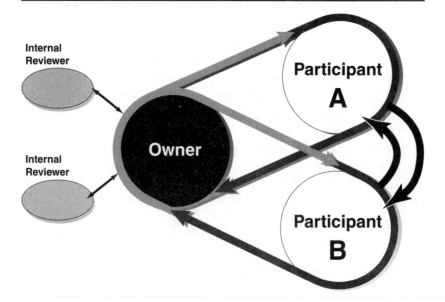

important for companies collaborating on product and process design, where there can be many players involved, and where the precision of drawings is crucial. In these cases, image distortion makes the fax a less-than-optimal communication medium; couriers are too slow and expensive when documents must be shipped to many parties; and e-mail is inefficient because of the size of technical specification sheets, computer-aided design (CAD) drawings, and other design documentation.

Reducing Cost

The enterprise community workplace lowers the total cost of process ownership by reducing the time, effort, and financial cost of moving ideas and concepts—as well as the documentation for those ideas and concepts—around the network of collaborators. It reduces the training costs for partners by providing easy-to-use interfaces for communications; collaborators no longer need to know how to use a host of different systems. Finally, especially when combined with video conferencing technology, the workplace enables rapid problem resolution and decision making. It also reduces the cost of travel, especially on complex project collaboration where face-to-face dialogue is very important.

COLLABORATIVE ENGINEERING AND PROJECT MANAGEMENT: USING THE ENTERPRISE COMMUNITY WORKPLACE

Today, time-to-market is one of the most important drivers of product development. But, when dealing with large numbers of disbursed business partners up and down the supply chain, companies—especially large global companies—face the physical limitations imposed by time and distance. In some cases, virtual companies exist where an original equipment manufacturer (OEM) or the project owner becomes the assembly point for components received from global outsourcing partners.

To cope with these limitations, enterprises must create infrastructures that facilitate product development efficiency by better involving both customers and all of the external business partners in the development process, thereby integrating product design with the overall planning, sourcing, and execution processes. In this way, product configuration can be managed from development through production and service. The Internet provides the ideal enabling technology for creating such an infrastructure. It reduces the time needed to bring people together and lets them exchange their knowledge and ideas efficiently, independent of their physical locations.

Workplace Solution from Enterprise and Partner Perspectives

Let us look at a collaborative engineering scenario from the perspectives of two roles: (1) the project manager within the project-owner organization, and (2) a developmental engineer within a partner organization.

The project manager's business problem is framed by the following question: "How can I effectively communicate with my suppliers and partners on a project?" The three-fold solution to the problem involves:

1. An overview of the project status through a means of sharing project plans and status reports among all partners.
2. A way to provide partners with all the information they need to work on the project in a structured manner.
3. A way to reconcile all partners' inputs and changes.

The following question frames the business problem of a development engineer from outside the organization: "How can I reduce administrative overload—phone calls, faxes, and the paperwork necessary to obtain information—and effectively communicate my ideas and results to the other parties involved in the project?" This problem also requires a three-fold solution involving:

1. The ability to obtain an overview of all projects that are in the queue and of who does/did what on which project.
2. Access to all related information such as plans, project structures, and the ability to take the work offline. (This

material cannot simply be a group of files; rather, it must be a structured database that facilitates making changes simultaneously with others who are designing components that are integrally tied to and affected by the changes made to the component on which this engineer is working.)

3. An environment that allows the engineer to inform all other participants involved of the changes being made.

Business Benefits

The business benefits of such a workplace-based system are clear:

- The shorter turn-around time for communication exchanged among design and engineering partners improves time to market.
- Cooperation is easy, and, therefore, improved. With extensible markup language (XML) data exchange (which can be used only if partners have agreed to a common standard) collaborators are not constrained by specific system requirements. The collaboration is independent of each partner's internal computer systems. There is no permanent online system access required, so work can be taken off line. Security is provided within the communication medium; no partner's internal systems have to be opened to other partners. A new virtual company can be created on the fly for each project. Entities are not required to maintain the relationship longer than for the duration of the project.
- Costs are minimized because there is no need to train collaborating partners on the project owner's specific computer systems.
- The process is managed effectively because push technology drives monitoring of project goals and key performance indicators for both the project owner and each participant.

A Day in the Life of the Enterprise Community Workplace: Collaborative Engineering

A manufacturer of anti-lock brake systems (ABS) has just been awarded a contract to design a system for a new automobile. The design engineer who will manage the project needs to work closely with the design engineers from three other companies that are developing sub-assemblies for the ABS. The project manager also needs to communicate the current status of the project with the client to verify acceptance and check for conformance with contract specifications.

Figure 7.5 illustrates the workplace of an individual managing a collaborative engineering project. The workplace includes a launching area on the left side from which he or she can access detailed information or applications, as well as a host of mini-applications residing on the right side. Many of these show project tracking data that the project manager needs constantly. This information is being pushed to the project manager by the system.

On the workplace, the project manager creates a configuration folder by going to the collaboration section of the launching area. This folder holds all relevant information, including the parts lists, CAD models for the various subassemblies, the overall project plan, and the client's specification documents. In addition to the basic dates of the project planning board, he or she also publishes the e-mail addresses of the three engineers who are project managers at partner facilities.

All partners receive an e-mail notification confirming their participation in the project and outlining the process for communicating. The e-mail includes the link to the project folder where the project work will be housed. This guides partners to the project owner's Web site and information repository. Each project team member uses a Web browser to retrieve the current project information assigned to them.

The project manager creates a basic proposal for the ABS system by using the engineering workbench and then sends it to all of the partners. They modify it as necessary to conform to their designs for the particular component for which they are responsible. All modifications are made within the configuration folder and are available to all of the partners and to the project manager.

Figure 7.5   A Workplace for Collaborative Engineering

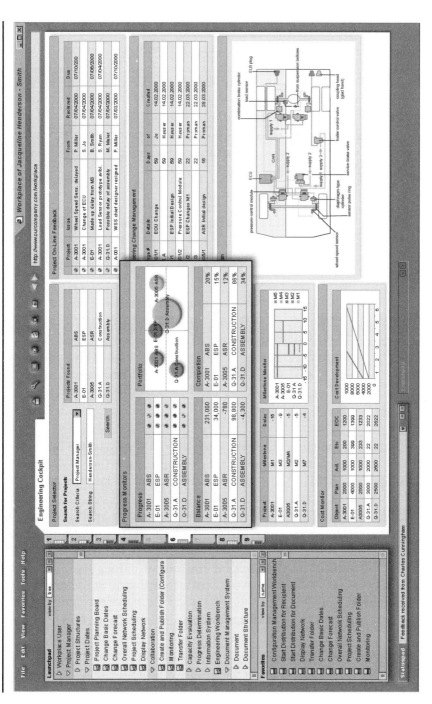

113

Since all parties can view the same design documents, meetings can be held online to discuss open design issues. If a change to the project plan is made in the project planning board, it is communicated to all. If at some point in the effort a milestone is delayed, the project planning board communicates this change immediately to everyone in the collaborative network.

Figure 7.6 illustrates a simple four-step project lifecycle flow for this design work, from formulating the idea to communicating the final design to the client.

1. The project owner creates a design proposal, submits it via the community workplace, and issues an e-mail notification to partners that the design is available.
2. Partners receive notice, follow the link to the workplace, and retrieve project information.
3. Each partner has an opportunity to make changes to the design and comment on changes previously made by other partners.
4. Finally, the project owner reconciles the changes, compares various modifications, checks the consistency of the updated design, and forwards the new design to the client.

Both the client and the partners have access to the project via a link. The client can download the contents of the configuration folder and work off line. After reviewing the design, the client can comment and even mark up the drawings. These comments can then be uploaded to the project owner's server again. All project participants receive the same set of requests for modifications from the client.

In addition to the tools for collaborative design, a community workplace for business partner collaboration must include a suite of tools the project owner can use to track project progress, review and compare the work of various business partners, and reconcile the results. The project manager needs to have an on-line status inbox to view incoming responses from various business partners and internal project participants and a tool for tracking due dates on all current projects under his or her control.

Figure 7.6 Project Life-Cycle Flow

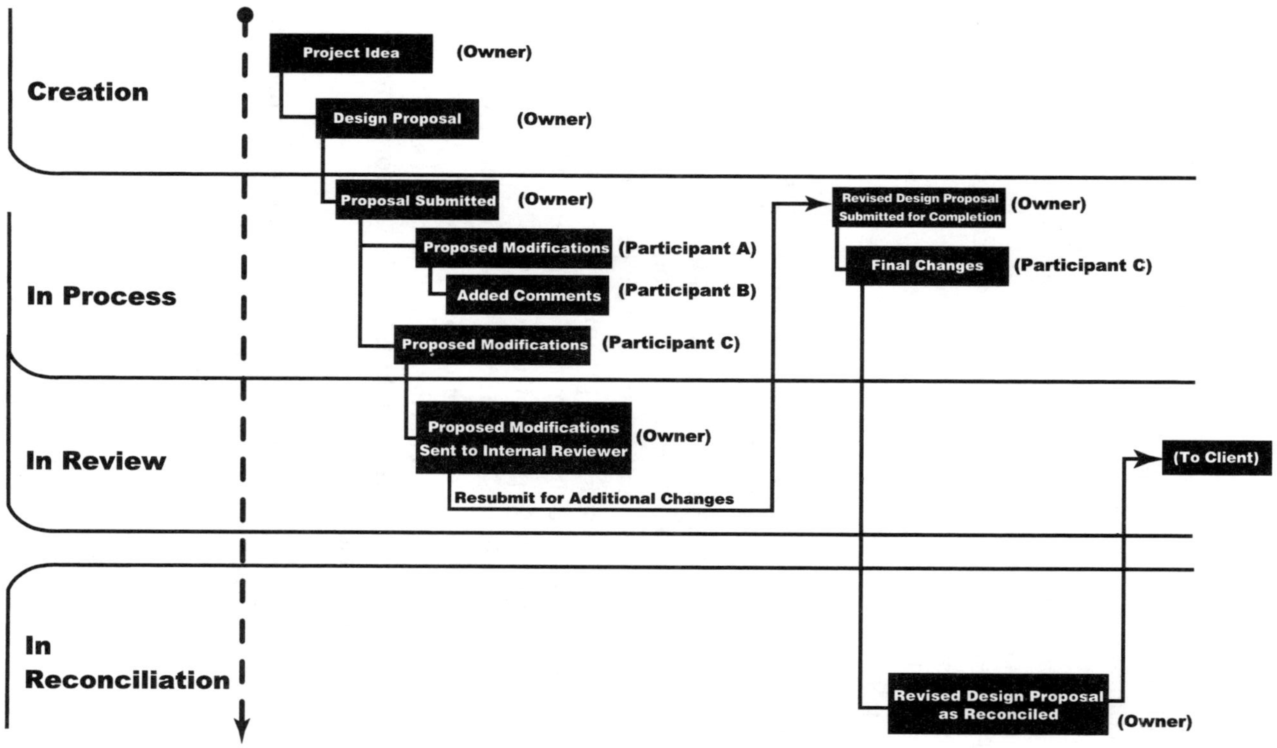

With the project selector, the project manager gets an overview of all of his or her projects. The project monitors are automatically updated to show all key performance indicators for each project's progress. These might include overall status, cost, and milestone tracking. This information is important to the project manager's communication with the customer, who might request status reports.

Feedback is pushed to the workplace allowing the project manager to compare and reconcile all of the possible changes. The same technology allows the project manager to obtain a quick overview of the engineering changes to date. Using drag-and-relate technology, the project manager can pull details from the corresponding section on the launching area.

COLLABORATIVE PLANNING: USING THE ENTERPRISE COMMUNITY WORKPLACE

Collaborative planning involves individuals inside the enterprise as well as customers, suppliers, distributors, third-party logistics providers and/or installers, and service personnel.

To enable collaborative planning, an e-business uses Internet connectivity for real-time communication and advanced planning across multiple enterprises. This connectivity synchronizes product flow and optimizes resource allocation resulting in either one-to-one or hub-based collaboration (Figure 7.7). In a hub-based collaboration model, all participants have equal and timely access to the same information. A hub-based collaboration model includes five key elements:

1. Collaborative forecasting-to-replenishment between trading partners and manufacturers
2. Collaborative agreement-to-forecast for standardized components between suppliers and manufacturers
3. Real-time inventory visibility and constraint planning across the supply chain
4. Dynamic plant loading and rescheduling across manufacturing and supplier plants
5. Real-time available-to-promise (ATP).

Figure 7.7   E-Business Enabled Collaborative Planning

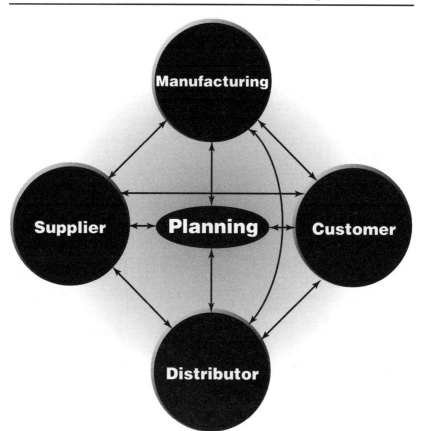

All members of a community workplace have real-time access to demand, forecast, and production data and all benefit from an optimized supply chain, reduced time to market, increased customer loyalty, improved customer service, and more explicit cost management. The enterprise and all of its suppliers also benefit from reduced inventory carrying and obsolescence costs, supply-chain cycle time, and order-replenishment lead time; improved capacity utilization, visibility of demand, and replenishment and inventories data across the supply chain; and from on-time delivery.

Three Views of the Workplace

Each of the three participant types in the workplace—the customer, the enterprise, and the supplier—uses it in a different way.
The customer is able to change forecasts and demand on the
enterprise by creating, adjusting, and canceling orders, and by
changing configuration or delivery requirements. When creating
a new order, the customer can obtain real-time available-to-
promise information, as well as product information and production schedules. The customer also tracks production and delivery
of product.

The enterprise uses this customer information to integrate
forecasts and demand and to establish and manage production
schedules across the enterprise and the various suppliers in a way
that enhances capacity utilization and tailors the supply chain.
Process and project owners within the enterprise also use the
workplace to establish and maintain collaboration agreements
with various partners and to manage collaborative design efforts.

Suppliers use the enterprise workplace to manage better the
movement of goods to (and any inventory the supplier is managing
for) the enterprise. The supplier can track forecasts and demand
and update inventory availability for the enterprise and any other
suppliers it feeds with components for subassembly. The supplier
also uses the workplace to update component design information
and to participate more closely in product-design efforts.

Collaborating Workplaces

In a world where many large, global companies are using workplace technology, a logical question emerges: "Where does the
collaborative work happen?" The answer is, it happens in the workplace of the company that "owns" the business process underlying
any given transaction.

In our example, the car design would take place in the car
company's workplace. But once the car company has contracted
with a Tier 1 supplier to design and produce an anti-lock braking
system, the design would take place in the supplier's workplace,
since it owns the design process. Collaborators would work within
the designer's workplace until the design is completed. At that

point, the Tier 1 supplier would feed the design documentation into the car company's workplace.

In the above example, integration among workplaces is the key to success. The program manager (that is, the individual at the car company who is heading up the design team) must be able to see a "roll up" of all the work being accomplished in the various component suppliers' workplaces. The car company must have access to information about the state of affairs at each of the major component suppliers. In other words, multiple workplaces designed by multiple technology providers must feed information into the car company's workplace. Only then will the program manager be able to access up-to-date information from each supplier—information based on the work being done by collaborators in each supplier's workplace.

A Day in the Life of the Enterprise Community Workplace: Collaborative Planning

A major customer has canceled an order, forcing the enterprise and all other participants in the enterprise community workplace to change their forecasts and their activities. This event, depicted in Figure 7.8, reverberates through the workplace and the technology sends the appropriate cues and unique messages to each participant.

Figures 7.9 through 7.11 illustrate a series of messages sent to all the supply web participants involved in a simple event: a customer cancels an order. In this case, only three messages are sent.

1. The customer receives confirmation that the order is cancelled.
2. The third-party logistics provider receives a message to cancel delivery and to return any items in storage.
3. Suppliers receive messages asking them to respond to an updated production schedule.

Now, let us consider a more complex event: An installer surveys an equipment installation site and discovers that the customer will not be prepared to receive the equipment on the agreed upon delivery date. The workplace—possibly accessed through a mobile

Figure 7.8   An Event Can Be Communicated to All Participants in a
Collaborative Planning Model

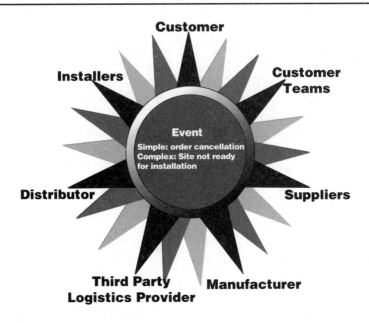

Figure 7.9   Message to Customer

Figure 7.10   Message to Third-Party Logistics Provider

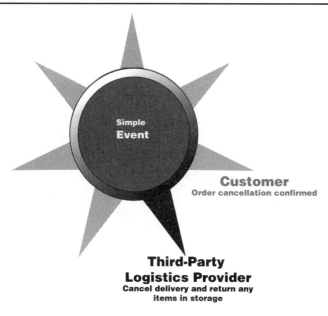

Figure 7.11   Messages to Suppliers

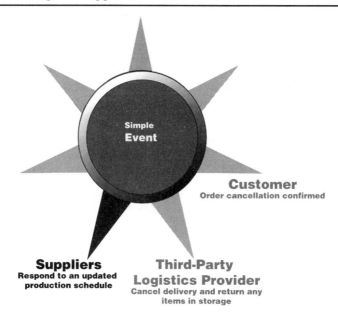

Figure 7.12   Message to Manufacturer

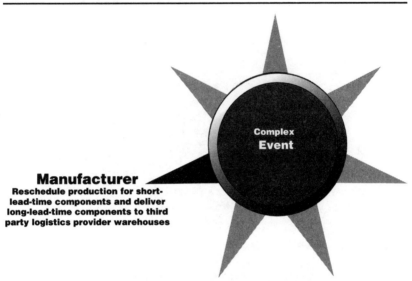

device—informs others in the network of the project delay and verifies availability of resources and materials for a revised installation date.

In this instance, four messages go out to participants (Figures 7.12 through 7.15):

1. The manufacturer (a business unit of the core enterprise) receives a message to reschedule production for short-lead-time components and to deliver long-lead-time components to the third-party logistics provider's warehouse.

2. The third-party logistics provider receives a message to schedule pick-up of long-lead-time items for storage in the warehouse and to schedule pick-up and delivery of short lead-time components to the site, with in-transit merge of items stored in the warehouse.

3. Suppliers receive messages to reschedule delivery of raw materials, based on production changes, and to reschedule delivery of materials being directly shipped to the site.

4. Finally, the customer receives confirmation of a new installation start date.

Figure 7.13   Message to Third-Party Logistics Provider

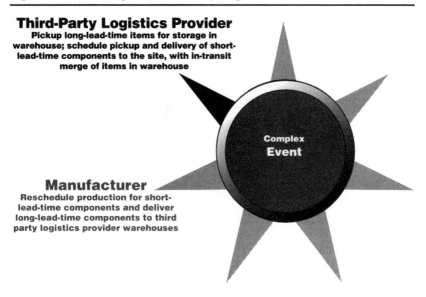

Figure 7.14   Messages to Suppliers

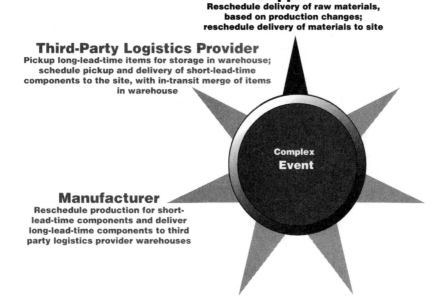

Figure 7.15   Message to Customer

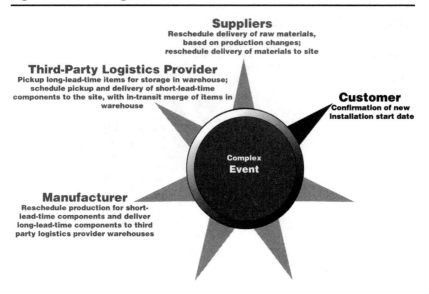

Workplace Benefit

The workplace for each member of the collaborative planning web is the access point to a single supply chain planning and management system. Communication and information are seamless, real time, and responsive. The work among the partners is dynamic rather than sequential. No longer merely the start of a chain of information exchange, an event triggers information to flow out to all affected parties. By utilizing workflow within the workplace, each event can be the trigger for a carefully coordinated, automated flow of work to the relevant parties participating in the supply web. This web flow, or workflow over the Web, drives the process flow such that it becomes transparent where the work item originated. Information about events and the status of the supply web is open to all members of the collaborative community. Faster response to changes and more accurate planning lead to reduced cost for all members of the web and better service to the end customer.

The workplace can be easily reconfigured to accommodate new suppliers, logistics providers, and other partners because a

Web browser and Internet connectivity are the only technical requirements for entry into the supply web. Training is not needed and support is universal. The workplace shields members of the collaborative unit from the technology behind it (whether this is a single system controlled by the hub enterprise or multiple systems working together).

8

Workplace Technology

A flexible architecture that integrates with an existing system landscape is required to build a workplace for each individual employee or external user. A workplace serves as an open integration
platform that combines data and information from different technical components and drives interaction with the individual.

Figure 8.1 categorizes workplace and e-business components.
A Web browser or other device visualizes the workplace content.
The workplace server drives the collection of content and its role-
based and personalized presentation. Information, applications,
and services either can be accessed directly or via the workplace
server. In the case of direct access, the workplace serves as an organizational tool; in the case of access via the workplace server,
data and information are combined from several components,
and the individual receives enriched, value-added content.

Understanding this architecture requires familiarity with the
system's function. An individual sits in front of a computer. The
computer is running a Web browser (the workplace front end)
through which the individual has access to a myriad of information and application sources. All of this content is provided by
"component systems" and consists of documents, services, transactions, etc. Some content resides on servers or mainframes inside
the company. Other content resides on servers or mainframes operated by other companies, such as third-party software providers,
business partners, or Web service providers. Examples of content
supplied by the application component include all e-business

Figure 8.1 Workplace and E-Business Components

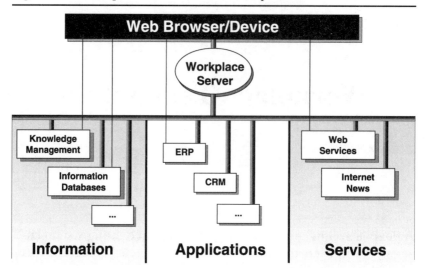

applications for customer relationship management, supply chain management, e-commerce, business intelligence, and ERP or other generic applications. For example, file servers, Web servers, news group servers, and document/mail management systems such as Lotus Notes and Microsoft Exchange provide information content. The workplace gives each individual access to all of the systems inside the company as well as to external systems.

The tasks of the workplace server fall into two categories. On the one hand, the workplace supports intrinsic management capabilities such as user management (including authentication and security), role management (including a directory of the content available to the roles and the mapping of users and roles), navigation facilities such as drag and relate, and personalization services for design and content. On the other hand, the workplace serves as an open integration platform, collecting and adding value to the content, and facilitating the interaction of individuals with business processes. Thus, the workplace provides an integration layer that hides the heterogeneous information and application system landscape both inside and outside the company.

TYPICAL INTERACTION WITH THE WORKPLACE

In a typical interaction with the workplace, an individual logs on via the Web browser to the workplace server. The workplace server authenticates the individual and subsequently grants access to all content that his or her role is authorized to use. This process is called single sign-on.

After log-on, the workplace server delivers to the individual his or her personal workplace, which consists of an overall layout, look, and feel, and which is usually specific to the company and the individual rather than to the workplace software vendor. The individualized workplace contains a launch area that offers the applications, information, and services appropriate to the individual's specific role(s). This launch space is often called the "pull area" since the user has to "pull" information or activate the system. A workplace also contains "push areas" through which information is pushed to the individual. The user might have requested this information when he or she personalized the workplace, or the information can originate with corporate, business unit, or departmental leadership who want it pushed to individuals who act in particular roles.

From the launch area, the individual accesses all of the information, applications, and services to which he or she has access rights. These can include e-mail; personal productivity tools like word processing, spreadsheets, and graphics; a universal workflow inbox containing work items from all system components; the company's e-business applications, applications held on remote servers within the enterprise, and external Web services and applications from other companies that are accessible over the Internet. All of this is in the Web browser and, to the person using the workplace, appears as a single, coherent system. The component landscape is completely transparent, and the individual worker needs to know nothing about it to get his or her job done.

The workplace serves as an open integration platform. Integration of component systems can be accomplished in two ways. Individuals either directly access the existing component systems or the workplace aggregates the data and information available in the existing component systems and provides a new user interaction experience. Direct access is easier to achieve and covers all types of interaction. Aggregation, however, requires more effort but potentially provides more benefit and value-added service. A workplace should support both types of integration. Companies must always weigh effort against benefit in deciding which integration method to use.

WORKPLACE FEATURES

A workplace consists of nine main technical features:

1. Security
2. Presentation integration of component systems
3. Integration of information sources and documents
4. Search and Web content management
5. Web application development and workflow
6. Roles
7. Workplace builder
8. Personalization
9. Administration.

Security

Today, every component system has its own user management tools, log-in procedures, and directory of services. One of the ways to ensure a successful workplace—one that saves time and enhances productivity—is to unify system access by unifying log-on procedures and directories. To do this, four basic security measures must be embedded in the workplace: authentication, single sign-on, authorization, and auditability. Security issues exist both within the workplace itself and across the network.

Authentication

The authentication process ensures that the user is who he or she claims to be. Several authentication technologies are available, including login and password, certificates, smartcard, and physical evidence (finger print, retina scan). A workplace must interface with all of the authentication processes the various systems use.

Authentication in any technical form "lives" in each system's user management logic; that is, the user must be known in each component system.

The technology placed inside the workplace server, however, must integrate all of these various authorizations. Implementing authentication—getting the old systems to "play along" with the workplace—is, sometimes, a tricky technical feat because of the lack of standards.

Single Sign-On

Once authenticated, the individual at the workplace needs secure access to all of the systems that, at least in principle, feed into it. The problem is getting the enterprise's various internal and external servers to "understand" the single sign-on emanating from the workplace server. Digital certificates with a public key infrastructure accomplish this objective and serve as a standard authentication technique. In the future, most component systems, including mainframe components and all Web sites, will be extended to support these standard authentication mechanisms. For existing components, add-on solutions that integrate with a public key infrastructure will be broadly available. For example, after authentication, users are provided with a "ticket" that grants access to the integrated component systems for the time the individual is logged onto the workplace. Components can be easily integrated in a ticketing infrastructure by integrating ticketing libraries into the components.

Authorization

Authorization defines what an individual can do, start, or access, once he or she has been authenticated by a component system. Workplace authorization controls only general access to a particular system. Each component system will have additional authorization checks. All system security cannot be delegated to the workplace. The workplace can control what an individual can do based on that person's role. But each component system must add an additional layer of authorization with respect to the specific actions an individual can take while working in the system.

For instance, an accounts payable clerk, the manager of the accounts payable, and the controller may each be authorized to

ENCRYPTION AND CERTIFICATES

Traditionally, users log on to a system, that is, authenticate themselves through a log-on dialog that supplies a user ID and a password. This becomes a problem when the user works with many systems. In fact, the user may even have different log-on IDs for different systems. The question is this: How can an organization safely identify (authenticate) a user and then use this authentication information for several systems? Digital certificates that are directly supported by browsers and HTTPS (the secure Internet protocol based on secure socket layer (SSL)) offer one solution.

Digital identities are cryptographic keys (bitstreams) that use sophisticated mathematical protocols to identify their owners. To bind digital identities to persons or systems, a **trust center** issues a **certificate** that expresses trust in the digital identity of a person or system. One aspect of the digital identity, the so-called **private key**, always remains with the person, whereas another, the **public key**, is part of the certificate. Certificates, therefore, are, in a sense, digital passports.

To authenticate the (physical) identity of a person, the trust center relies on the approval of a **registration authority** that actually checks the person's identity. Depending on the rigor of the check, different **classes** of certificates check different things. For example, one class of certificates might check the correctness of an e-mail address; another, the physical presence of an individual at an office.

If many persons receive a certificate, and if they trust the service of the trust center, they form a hierarchical trust community called a **public key infrastructure** (PKI). Different public key infrastructures are disjointed by default; where the level of trust needs to be high, mechanisms must be established for expanding trust over more than one PKI (**cross certification, certification validation service**).

Certificates can be used for **authentication, digital signatures**, and **encryption**. Since certificate-based authentication has been standardized and is supported by standard browsers, it can be used for both company-wide secure single sign-on and secure log on of partners using the company's portal. Digital signatures can be used for equipping transactions within a company or cross-company with **integrity, authenticity**, and **non-repudiation**. Certificates could also be used for **secure e-mail** (digital signatures and encryption), but the management effort is much higher than for authentication and digital signatures.

The distribution of certificates within a company or to its partners is very different from one PKI to another. For example, Identrus is an international banking consortium's PKI that requires every person to register physically at the bank and to use a **smart card**. The mySAP Workplace Trust Center Service uses software certificates and takes advantage of automatic certificate enrollment for company employees and partners.

access the accounts payable module of the company's ERP system. But, because of their different roles, each has a different level of authorization to change data in the system. In another example, a clerk in the personnel office can change certain salaries, but not his or her own and not that of the person for whom he or she works.

Thus, fine-grained authorization must take place within the component systems. The workplace authorization performs only a part of a complete authorization process that the component system must complement. For example, individuals who are not authorized to perform certain tasks can get around workplace authorization by asking friends who possess the authorization to e-mail them the restricted uniform resource locator (URL) for accessing this functionality. Such security holes must be eliminated, and authentication by the component system must be enforced. In fact, every request to a component system must be authenticated if access is restricted. Depending on the level of authorizations granted, each request must be checked by the different component

systems. The workplace cannot completely manage all authorizations. To do so would require replicating the entire business logic
on the application.

Auditability

The workplace can provide legally binding evidence to prove who
gained access to what system at what time; who started work within
what system; and at what time a person began using a particular
system. But it cannot determine or audit what was actually done
within the application—for example, which data was changed or
which transactions were recorded. Another level of auditing
within the application component is necessary to provide this information. Again, the audit function of the workplace duplicates
some aspects of the component systems. But only a two-tiered
audit provides the necessary comprehensive information. Additionally, it is necessary to confirm that a component system user
and a user on the workplace are the same individual who might
have multiple user identifications within the different system
components.

Network Security

Besides access, the data and information transferred during access
need to be secured, and privacy between the individual and the
component system needs to be enforced. This is handled on the
network layer via secure network communication. Network security is accomplished by encrypting both communication and content across systems and, more importantly, across company
boundaries. When companies use the workplace to collaborate
with business partners, neither party must be able to breach the
other's system security walls, even by accident.

   Integrating third-party components enables a secure network
communication to be established. Even when communicating
over the open Internet a secure network communication can be
established with support of virtual private networks (VPNs). The
classic Internet protocol (HTTP) also has a secure variant called
HTTPS that ensures encrypted secure communication and that is
a standard supported by all Web browsers.

Security Checklist

When evaluating workplace software, companies should consider the following with respect to security:

- User Management and Authentication
  - What user management tools does the workplace provide?
  - What interfaces does it provide to integrate with other authentication tools?
- Single Sign-On
  - What systems does the company use?
  - What needs to be done to the systems to utilize single sign-on?
  - Do the systems understand X.509 certificates, or do they use a proprietary standard?
  - Does the workplace software support certificates? Does it support other ways (interfaces) to accomplish single sign-on?
- Network Security
  - Is standard secure network communication supported?
  - Can secure access over the Internet be supported?

Presentation Integration of Component Systems

Web browsers display content in HTML and can run Java applets (little programs that have a distinctive visual appearance in the browser). But most existing systems do not "speak" HTML; rather, they use other communication protocols—for example, standard terminal protocols, such as vt220, IBM 3270, or XWindows. Other component systems require client-server configurations where the application runs on a server but special client front-end software is needed to access the application—software that must be installed on desktops or laptops.

   A distinction must be made between integrating component systems that reside on other servers and local applications that reside on desktop PCs because these are still today two separate and distinct computing platforms.

Integrating Server Components

To integrate all of the company's component systems fully—that is, to allow all of these systems to appear on an individual's Web-based front end— a workplace must support a set of standard presentation integration tools. Examples of these are terminal server gateways, such as Citrix, XWindows, or pcAnywhere, and emulations such as those for vt220 and IBM 3270 systems.

Workplace architecture designers and implementers must answer three questions:

1. Which systems does the company currently use?
2. Which of those require gateways or adapters?
3. Which gateways require separate servers to operate and which can be run directly in the browser? (For example, a Citrix terminal requires a separate server, while a 3270 emulator Java applet runs directly in the Web browser.)

Integrating Local Applications

Most individuals still use a desktop PC as a standard device on which many other locally installed tools are located. A workplace should also integrate all of these locally available tools, that is, those that typically reside on each individual PC rather than on a server or mainframe. These include e-mail software, calendar tools, and office applications, among others.

Many of these are locally installed "client" applications that work in conjunction with "server" applications. Here the workplace must offer a means to integrate, for example, a local mail application so that it can run directly in the browser. This, however, still requires local/client installations on the PC. The "local" applications show up on the workplace as components or MiniApps along with the information, applications, and services that come from various internal and external systems. In addition, collaboration tools need to be integrated into the workplace to leverage fully the user's ability to work with suppliers, customers, and other business partners.

Increasingly, these tools are also available for direct use in a Web browser, eliminating the need to install all client tools on each desktop PC. Examples include Internet mail services available through consumer portals such as Hotmail or Yahoo!, or typical Web-based discussion groups. These run completely in the browser and no client software needs to be installed on the desktop PC.

Session Handling

In the consumer Internet world, where individuals use so-called dead pages or read-only material, a server can handle hundreds, if not thousands, of concurrent users. But in the world of transaction-based live pages and dialogs, individuals work in sessions. A session is a sequence of pages/dialog steps that logically belong together to perform a certain task with a definite start and end. In contrast to just viewing items but leaving them unchanged, users working with business processes that have defined start and end states change or update data on the server. Sessions are the heart of the Internet. However, maintaining a session on a server requires a lot of computing resources. If an individual exits a particular application without going through the proper exit protocol, resources remain engaged, which is very expensive. All the server can do is close the session and release the resources after a fixed amount of time.

A typical session on a Web application server involves a sequence of requests and responses unique to that session. The pages belonging to the same session (and thus the same user) are kept together by a session identification (ID) in the form of a "cookie" or as part of a URL. This standard session-ID technology exists for standard Web platforms. When a user completes a session, dialog, or task and chooses the "commit," "save," or "done" button, the server releases the resources that had been used for that session.

Typical e-business applications that reside in a company's systems environment require large amounts of available resources during a sequence of dialog steps that form, for example, a transaction or that involve interactive reporting or data mining. Clearly, such sessions need to be carefully managed.

Consider an individual running an application in a browser. What if he or she leaves in the middle of a transaction or even closes the browser? Since HTTP is a connection-less protocol, the server never discovers that the individual does not intend to finish the transaction. Thus, the server must always keep resources available to accommodate a generous time-out period, tying up server resources and severely impacting scalability and performance. After the end of the time out, the server finishes the session and the individual can no longer complete the task. He or she is not informed about the possibility of losing unfinished work. To enhance user interaction and provide more scalability and higher performance, session management capabilities are needed. With such capabilities, individuals can manage several sessions in parallel and are not forced to complete their jobs in single sessions. Providing access to a wide variety of e-business applications utilizing browser technology without sophisticated session-management technology is not recommended. Legacy system integration cannot provide session management. The workplace—the enterprise portal—must provide session management (the ability to run and maintain several sessions in parallel) to allow true presentation integration of component systems and the ability to run them in the browser. The best enterprise portal technology has in place software that cues the individual in his or her workplace to close out a session that is tying up server resources.

Presentation Integration of Component Systems Checklist

When implementing a workplace, a company needs to understand both its existing systems and how different workplace software supports integration of those systems. Answering the following questions aids in achieving that understanding:

- What kinds of systems does the company have?
  - Do the systems have direct http/HTML access?
  - What gateways are available?
  - Can standard integration tools like Java applets be used?
  - Do company systems understand digital certificates for single sign-on?
  - Can gateways and Web application servers understand session handling?
- Does the workplace software allow integration of local tools, such as e-mail and collaboration tools?

— Does the workplace software integrate server-based Web tools to avoid local installation?

— Does the workplace software support integration of locally installed applications and tools?

— What local collaboration tools are being used in the company (e.g., Lotus Notes, Microsoft Exchange)? Is the workplace software capable of "calling" them?

Integration of Information Sources and Documents

In addition to accessing application components, a workplace must also provide ways to access knowledge that is often available as documents in various formats that reside in a large variety of databases, file servers, and local Web sites or in dedicated document management systems such as, for example, Lotus Notes and Microsoft Exchange. Before integrating these information sources and documents, they must first be accessed and visualized in the workplace environment.

To ensure seamless access capabilities in a workplace environment, the documents should be accessible via a URL. Increasingly, file servers support URL access. If documents are stored in specialized document servers, interfaces must be available that allow accessing these documents via URLs.

Documents accessed via URLs also need to be viewed. If the documents are available in HTML format, they can be visualized in a Web browser. Otherwise, either server-based converters in HTML or plug-ins that visualize the document in Web browsers can be deployed. Web browser plug-ins for viewing documents are available for portable document files (PDFs) and office documents such as the ones created with text processing tools. These have to be installed locally and typically require one plug-in per document type.

Search and Web Content Management

The corporate knowledge that is hidden in a large variety of sources and document formats is typically unstructured. The right information for the right task, therefore, is not always available when needed. Individuals spend large amounts of time searching for this knowledge. Support of search capabilities is mandatory in a workplace environment.

Computer users search all the time, and searching is one of the most expensive tasks they perform. A large company may have thousands of file and Web servers containing many kinds of documents. The task of a workplace search engine is to integrate these documents, index them, and make them accessible to all appropriate users in a cost-effective manner.

Most searches are conducted to find Information used for decision-making. Good searches lead to better and faster decisions. Making searching more efficient and effective is one of the key goals of implementing workplace technology and can result in major financial benefits.

Searches are undertaken in different ways for different purposes. Some searches are for unstructured information located in documents; others are for data from reports and for query-structured data such as on-line analytical processing (OLAP) analysis. Still others involve queries concerning objects in databases. There are different ways to search for the same information, and users have different preferences about how they search.

The workplace must support powerful, integrated searches and different ways to search, and its search capability must reach all kinds of content. An individual using a workplace should be able easily to specify sophisticated comprehensive searches (search programming).

Search engines and other search capabilities are usually not built into workplace software but are part of the enterprise portal offering. Therefore, the workplace's ability to integrate with existing search tools is critically important. Additionally, the workplace environment should integrate Web content management tools with search. It must be possible not only to conduct a full text search, but also to classify content to be searched. Ideally, individuals must be able to publish content. They must be able to classify documents via attributes either manually or automatically based on the content of the document. This supports building a corporate taxonomy and filling this taxonomy with real documents and allows them to be transformed into knowledge.

Search and Web Content Management Checklist

The following questions can help a company evaluate its search capability needs:

- What kind of content does the company have?
  — Does content include intranet pages, collaborative tools, graphics databases, streaming media, etc.?
- What search engine features does the workplace software offer?
  — What search engine does it support? Can it access all content for indexing?
  — Does it allow for indexing, automatic categorization, etc.?
  — Can it interface with other search engines (e.g., in database objects)?
  — Can it interface with existing search engines?

Web Application Development and Workflow

Merely accessing or searching existing components is not always sufficient. Aggregating data and information available in component systems can achieve huge business benefits and provide value-added services and interfaces. To design end-to-end business processes, people and components must be easy to connect and implementing dedicated interfaces must be supported. Workflow capabilities and Web application development support complete the features needed in a comprehensive workplace environment serving as an open integration platform.

Search facilities help mainly to access information and make knowledge available to everybody. However, flexible end-to-end business processes must also be designed and then connected to the people that use them. Fragmented business processes should be combined, and the right people must be integrated at the right time. Workflow capabilities facilitate the design of these end-to-end business processes, and tasks are pushed to users so that they can be instantly completed. The workplace must support easy-to-use workflow tools that allow end-to-end business processes to be instantly changed and deployed. Also, access to data and information—that is, to the business objects that are handled in the processes—needs to be part of the workplace infrastructure. An order fulfillment process, for example, might need to be integrated with a customer survey and a Web promotion. A workflow pushes the right tasks to the right people. Responsibilities and initiatives may change quickly and the process and workflow need to be changed accordingly. The workplace must contain a powerful workflow engine that is aware of individuals and their roles and of organizational status. The workflow must integrate with existing components and be able to access and update the business objects originating from the different component systems.

Some tasks benefit from a specialized user interface that provides an aggregated view of information and data originating in different component systems. For example, in a collaborative business process, the business partners may need a tailored view of company data and a streamlined user interface focusing on their needs. A dedicated Web application may best serve this purpose. The workplace must provide the tools necessary to develop these Web applications using standard Internet technology. Access to and the ability to update data on existing components and an intuitive Web application development environment must be part of a workplace.

Enterprise application integration (EAI) tools help to get the right information to the right components and, therefore, must be integrated in a workplace environment. However, a workplace environment does not replace EAI tools. A well-integrated component landscape makes the task of building Web applications much easier. Together, EAI and workplace solutions ensure that data is integrated (with EAI) and used by individuals (with the workplace).

Web Application Development and Workflow Checklist

Companies grappling with Web application development and workflow issues should consider the following questions:

- What are the most important business processes? Where is value-added aggregation beneficial? What are the most important business processes that need to change flexibly?
- What application integration facilities are supported? Can data and information from different component systems

be accessed and updated? Are standard protocols and
tools supported?

- Are workflow capabilities provided that allow easy, intuitive, and fast design, deployment, and change of end-to-end business processes?

- How easy is it to design individual Web-based user interfaces? Is a development environment included?

Roles

A role within a company is defined by a set of activities a worker
must carry out in order to perform a specific job. Each role contains links to a set of information services and applications that
logically work together to help the user perform the role's particular set of activities. With a workplace, these links can be forged in
a structured manner. For example, the sales manager described in
Chapter 5 needs links to sales activities and other information, applications, and services including monitoring, planning, opportunities, inquiries and quotations, orders, contracts, customers and
contacts, products, pricing, promotions, rebates, competition, and
marketplaces, among others.

An individual generally acts in several roles within a company
(e.g., employee, manager, member of a business unit, etc.). Also,
some roles may be transient, such as that of a participant in a particular project with a finite duration. A person may be assigned
roles, or roles may be constructed to conform to what a person
already does. In the workplace environment, a role corresponds
logically to a set of push and pull information services and applications that can be visualized on the front end and that is used by
the individuals assigned to that role to fulfill its tasks. In this way,
the user sees what he or she can do in a logically connected way. A
particular individual's set of push and pull items can be visualized,
extended, or contracted as that person is assigned to or relieved of
other roles.

Role Development and Delivery

Each component system should "publish" a directory of the services it offers and make it easily accessible. The system's internal logic knows what the component offers, assembles the offerings into packages available to various roles and role fragments, and delivers these packages to the workplace server. Roles themselves are assembled in the workplace server.

For example, the services necessary to carry out human resource management activities may reside on a number of systems. These various services are taken from the many systems on which they reside and unified into one role in the workplace server. The individual who fulfills that role no longer sees "different systems" when he or she uses the computer; rather, the person sees one logical package of services necessary to perform the human resource management functions for which he or she is responsible. Moreover, when a service is moved from one server to another, those affected need not be notified since they do not need to change their favorite usage habits.

The workplace server is the place where all roles are maintained and published. Combining services into roles and assigning users to roles occur on the workplace server rather than on the individual component systems.

An important question for companies is, Who is allowed to "publish" into a role (i.e., Who is allowed to change and update data and information)? Also the "role" of the role administrator needs to have respective authorizations. Consider, for example, the role of a chief executive officer (CEO). When a person prepares a new report that should be a part of the CEO's role, he or she should be able to publish this report into the CEO role at a certain place. However, it should not be possible for the staff person to change the role arbitrarily. Allowable changes must be controlled carefully.

Or consider another case where several people share the same role. They should be able to personalize that role by extending it in a certain way, for example, to incorporate useful resources for the job. These extensions might become part of the standard role. In this way, the role becomes a medium for sharing best practices and resources. In other words, people should be able to *enhance* their own roles but not *remove* items defined by the company, and changes must be limited to the role. Basically, role administration is a central as well as a distributed task. With respect to roles, the company defines on the workplace server who can change what.

Service and Role Directory

With the concept of roles in mind, let us consider the system landscape within a typical company. The company has many component systems that each perform one or several business functions.

Each component system offers services—things they can do—such as human resources reporting or accounts payable processing. In order to publish these services to the workplace, they must be accessible—preferably rendered in HTML—and "callable" by a URL. This can also be accomplished by using an IBM 3270 applet or another adapter that can run directly in the browser.

The service and role directory is a repository for the services and roles in the workplace server and presents them in a logical organizational structure. The repository is an open directory for viewing, but writing to it is restricted by security controls.

Roles can be developed using tools outside the workplace, "published," and then made available to the workplace server. Individuals cannot unilaterally change their roles and thereby access restricted components, but they can personalize their workplaces in order to retrieve, in their "favorite" way, information, applications, and services from the components to which they have access.

The workplace creates a new set of menus and authorizations for the individual in any new role into which he or she is placed. In addition, the information, applications, and services necessary to fulfill a project role can be added to the person's menu at the beginning of the project's life and later deleted without altering the basic roles.

Roles Checklist

Companies involved in role issues should consider the following questions:

- Does the workplace incorporate the role concept?
- Does the workplace incorporate a powerful service/role directory? Does it support distributed authoring/publishing of roles?
- Does the role directory allow distributed administration/changes under the control of authorizations?

Workplace Builder

A company designing and implementing a workplace needs to think about the "workplace builder" (sometimes referred to as "portal builder") features it will offer on its front end, including the company's colors and logo, and possibly icons that have specific meaning within the company's culture.

Most companies want the look and feel of their workplaces to reflect their brand images and corporate cultures. This is easily accomplished with a workplace builder and tools such as cascading style sheets (CSS) that can change colors, positions, and icons, and workplace design tools that can change overall layout. Furthermore, a workplace environment should be multi-lingual and support several languages and character sets. A typical workplace should contain the following visual components:

- A "navigation" or "launch" area that contains navigational links and visualizes the pull portion of roles. This can be displayed in a tree structure or on Yahoo!-type link pages.
- A "home" area that displays content that is pushed out from the system or automatically distributed to all people who have asked for such information or to those who must have it to do their jobs. Companies can use their workplace to push company-wide information, strategic business-unit-wide information, or information that all people who fulfill a particular role need regularly. For instance, a sales manager may push out weekly sales figures by product or sales person to members of his or her sales force.
- A "work" area that displays documents and/or application interfaces individuals work on at any given time. The work area should be capable of displaying multiple workspaces and applications simultaneously.

Generally, several other "link areas" reside on the workplace. These link to information such as company and benefit news, subscribed folders and documents, predefined search results, individual favorites, etc.

An individual workplace should not be implemented by purchasing and installing an off-the-shelf product and using it without adapting it to specific company needs. A company must be able to customize its workplace to achieve the look and feel, layout, and content specific to its exact requirements. The best workplace technology product is the one that the company using the technology can most easily adapt.

Workplace Builder Checklist

A company analyzing workplace builder features should consider the following questions:

- With any given workplace product, how easy is it to achieve a specific layout, look, and feel?
- Does the workplace product include a builder tool, or will workplace building consist entirely of hand-coded project work?
- Does the workplace product support multiple languages?

Personalization

Personalization is user-specific adjustment of the visual appearance of the workplace, its content, or both. The degree to which the workplace can be personalized directly impacts user acceptance and workplace usefulness. The higher the degree of personalization, the greater the usefulness and acceptance by the user.

Workplace personalization can be achieved in several ways. First, the individual workplace view can be visually personalized. This includes the position of various tools, icons, and push area windows. In the same way that different individuals want their in-baskets, penholders, pending-action folders, and stacks of research/reading materials in different places on their desks, different people will want the virtual analogs of these physical items in different places on their computer workplace.

Users should be able to personalize content, that is to be able to add to their screens many content elements—termed Mini-Apps, gadgets, or portlets, depending on the vendor—and define their particular content. Examples include stock tickers, weather maps, mail inboxes, and news headlines, to name a few. Content that is pushed to the workplace front end can be treated in a number of ways. For example, a user could request that particular kinds of news be delivered as part of a news headline workplace feature. Content can also be personalized by location. For example, users might want to see daily weather and airport status reports for the cities in which they work or to which they frequently travel; or a user might engage an information agent to analyze and synthesize the information before it is pushed to the user.

Every application should be able to store some personalization settings in the workplace server and to load them when it is opened again. Users should be able to personalize their workplaces with ease. They should also be able to change content as frequently as they need or want to do so. Furthermore, some application components provide intrinsic personalization that is applied based on the fact that the user is authenticated. Personalization information that is stored on the workplace server or on the component to be integrated needs to be supported.

Personalization Checklist

The following questions about any workplace software's personalization capabilities need to be answered:

- How easily can look and feel be changed? Can an individual change the look and feel?
- How much can be changed? Can the content be changed?
- How easily can visual components such as colors, themes, and special menu trees be integrated?

Administration

Administration is a key item of a workplace's total cost of ownership. When comparing alternative workplace vendors, a company must evaluate the administration costs involved in each alternative.

The main workplace administration elements are:

- User management for authentication
- Role-based security and authorizations
- Integration of authorization between the workplace and the various component systems

- Continuous role development, deployment, and delivery
- Company branding.

The workplace software should enable central system administration for both individual users and roles and integration of roles and individuals. For example, it should be easy to assign users to roles, easy to change roles, and easy to integrate services from a component system into roles.

Another important issue is central user administration. The workplace should be able to integrate with existing user administration tools and share user data. Open standards are emerging that allow different systems to utilize the same user database so that the user really only needs one user identification and password for all systems. In the future, digital certificates will eliminate this need altogether. A workplace should be capable of accessing, importing, exporting, and synchronizing user data by supporting standard protocols such as, for example, the lightweight directory access protocol (LDAP) or directory services markup language (DSML).

TECHNICAL REQUIREMENTS OF THE WORKPLACE SYSTEM

When considering the installation of a workplace, companies must also address a number of important technical issues that may have an impact on cost. These include:

- System requirements
- Performance quality and scalability
- Federated architecture supporting several distributed workplace servers.

Each of these is defined by the answers to a set of questions.

System Requirements

The extent of hardware resources is one important aspect of workplace technical requirements.

Pertinent questions include:

- What are the system hardware/software requirements?
- How many people will the workplace host simultaneously?
- From how many different systems will the workplace consolidate applications?
- On what software platform should the workplace run (e.g., Windows NT, Unix)?
- What browser or browsers will the workplace support?
- What other devices—wireless, for example—should the workplace support?
- Is a network architecture needed that supports something besides TCP/IP?
- What are the associated software license fees?

Performance Quality and Scalability

Performance and scalability are also central issues. Good performance is key to user acceptance. Also, the workplace must be able to accommodate a large number of users and to expand capacity as a company grows. In addition to the workplace and related servers, network workload must also be considered. Pertinent questions include:

- What is the extent of the computing resources the average user will need?
- Should the workplace be available 24×7? What is the back-up plan if the server goes down?
- What is the plan for growth?
- How does the workplace scale?
- Does the design of the workplace portend performance bottlenecks?
- What are the workplace's network bandwidth requirements, and is this bandwidth necessary only for the intranet elements of the workplace or for outside participants as well?
- How many participants will use mobile devices?
- How many individuals access the workplace from outside the company (e.g., from home or on the road)?

Federated Architecture

In a federated architecture, distributed workplace servers can work together. This capability becomes quite important when, for example, a company installs a workplace for each division or strategic business unit, but, at least in theory, desires that all users be able to access all resources in all divisions (subject, of course, to authorizations). Pertinent questions include:

- Can many portal servers be connected?
- Can users be passed and/or shared among portal servers?
- Can the portal server interface with other user management tools (e.g., LDAP, other directories)?
- Can security mechanisms work together?
- Can search indices be integrated?

BEYOND THE BROWSER

Thus far, we have focused on the Web browser as the sole means of running and displaying information and application content on the workplace. However, the concepts discussed are equally applicable to other devices such as cell phones, personal digital assistants (PDAs), and set-top boxes (TV/computer combinations).

As new devices proliferate, Web application servers will need to support them by, for example, rendering information in wireless markup language (WML), rather than HTML. In fact, the workplace itself must become WML capable. The workplace will eventually have to support these new devices. When it does, it will know which parts of role content are accessible on what device and, supported by automatic conversion tools and more capable devices, more and more of the role content will also become accessible to the individual anytime, anywhere.

However, regardless of the device—and new devices will continue to evolve rapidly as others fall by the wayside—one fundamental principle remains unchanged: the workplace role concept will be increasingly critical to controlling the flood of information and choices that otherwise could easily become unmanageable for the working individual.

9

From Change Management to Manageable Change

In the new economy, where change is persistent, change management is an essential aspect of daily business. This environment calls for a reexamination not only of the methods traditionally used by corporate change managers, but also of the purpose of change management itself.

Change management no longer involves a discrete set of activities undertaken by sponsors, managers, and project staff in conjunction with a project or program that changes the way business is carried out (for example, process reengineering or systems implementation). Rather, because change is embedded in the daily work environment, change management must be rooted in the daily work of each and every manager and employee.

The workplace helps to turn this vision into reality. Because all employees use the workplace daily, change messages communicated through the workplace create an opportunity for a company to push out change information and action items to employees and to elicit their responses.

Figure 9.1 describes the difference between change management in a traditional systems implementation environment and change management in a workplace environment.

Figure 9.1 Change Management in Traditional versus Workplace Environments

	– Traditional environment	– Workplace environment
System characteristics	• Single-system focus • Project-by-project • Static	• Holistic • Role-based • Multi-system • Dynamic
Focus of change	• As-is to to-be • Process-based • System-focused • Misses work role	• People-focused • Role and content-based • Continuous worker involvement • Feedback loop
CM approach	• Extrinsic • Communication: why of change • Training: how of change • Reward and recognition reinforces use of system • System drives behavior	• Intrinsic • Enables change • Continuous learning • Learning builds knowledge • Reward and recognition based on meeting business objectives
Benefits of system change Benefits of CM support	• Process effectiveness and efficiency • System and process acceptance	• People effectiveness and efficiency • Achievement of business objectives

CHANGE MANAGEMENT TO DATE

Traditionally, change management involves moving an organization from one environment to another, taking the path of least resistance from the perspective of those affected by the change. In the technology environment, for instance, a key component of implementing an enterprise resource planning (ERP) system is a concurrent change management program designed to move users of the system from one technology environment to another while, at the same time, allaying their fears about how the system will affect their daily work. Such a program requires awareness, education, and specific training.

Change management focuses on helping employees move emotionally from an "as is" to a "to be" environment which, at the beginning of an undertaking, is merely a vision. In many instances, this involves moving from paper-based to PC-based operations, from individual work to teams, and/or from work performed within strategic business units (SBUs) to work accomplished within shared services. This model focuses on discrete changes. Although many elements might be rolled into the effort, it is executed as a single program (an event or series of events) designed to accomplish a single change.

In many technology implementations, people assigned to use the system have not previously been competent PC users, and moving from paper- to PC-based processes is, for them, a daunting task. The majority of users who have PC skills learned them through formal training or on the job; very few, if any, have "grown up" with computers as part of their daily lives. Corporate instructors have to lead large classes through step-by-step lesson plans that introduce both general PC concepts as well as aspects of the particular system. Such training is required to ensure user buy-in, the lack of which is often cited as a major roadblock to successful technology implementations.

Information generated in such change-management efforts is often static and specific to the underlying programmatic changes occurring in the working environment. Because it does not apply to broad, systemic organizational change, much of this information is lost when the project is completed.

Finally, change management is seen either as a cost or budget issue. Because it is viewed as a program with measurable outcomes to be carried out within a finite time, change management could be costed on a per-day or per-person basis. Funding is generally low and terminates with the successful implementation of the system. This means that day-to-day changes that occurred after the new system is operational—that is, after "go-live"—are often treated haphazardly because the change management team has been disbanded.

A change management program requires a number of resources, including experts in human resources, project management, process management, quality assurance, marketing, training, and, in the case of systems implementations, information technology (IT). To communicate change, management makes presentations to groups of employees and individuals receive a number of communications via company mail, desk drops, telephone follow-up and voice mail, email, and the company's intranet. These tools are adequate for static information—information that does not really live much longer than the time it takes to send it. In addition, such tools are disparate, forcing employees to look for change communications in many locations. Often, different regions, departments, or business units favor different tools, resulting in information that is not globally accessible and that different business units cannot leverage. In short, much of this material is out of date even before it hits the employee's inbox.

A typical change-management program has four parts:

1. Organizational change
2. Training
3. Communications
4. Reward and recognition.

While these elements are similar in any change management program, we discuss them here in the context of an ERP implementation in order to make a clear comparison between a project-oriented systems implementation and the holistic change necessary when moving to a workplace.

Organizational Change

As part of an organizational change program, change-management professionals examine what resources are needed to carry out the activities and processes that are being changed, identify existing resources whose roles encompassed these activities and processes, and design a "to be" organizational structure to meet the needs of the new activities and processes. Finally, within this organizational change model, the change-management professionals map the skills available across those needed. They hire individuals who possess those skills and retrain individuals whose skills are no longer necessary or sufficient to the newly designed activities and/or processes.

Training

In an ERP implementation, all people who are going to be using the system have to learn how to work within new processes. These are either based on prescribed best practices or customized. A system user has to learn step-by-step the particular ERP transactions specific to his or her job, including both the transaction process itself and the navigation of the ERP tools.

The amount of resources and time necessary to gear up the organization to use ERP generates much discussion about the logistics of training, including who should be trained in what, and when and where they should be trained. These discussions also center on development and distribution of training materials and electronic courseware, classroom PC set-ups, mapping processes to job roles and job descriptions, and a host of other issues. In short, training is costly, time intensive, and so focused on preparing people to use the ERP system that little time was left to train them in how to learn, grow, and adapt to rapidly changing technology.

In addition, some employees view training as an inconvenience and as time that can be spent more productively on "real" work. The most common training mode—instructor led, classroom based—does not allow for much flexibility in training delivery. Some people prefer to learn at their own pace, at their own desk—in short, in their own workplace—and do not feel comfortable asking questions in a classroom environment. Others simply pick up information at a faster pace and resent the time spent in the classroom. The instructor-led training model does not account for these individual differences; it is training for users rather than training for people.

Communications

Within an ERP change-management communications program, management messages are pushed to system users first to build their awareness of change and then to raise their change tolerance level. Senior corporate leadership handles awareness by taking "road shows" to remote facilities, while local management handles ongoing communication aimed at user acceptance.

Communication involves messages about why change was needed, what the "to be" environment will look like, and what will happen if change does not occur. The objective of many messages is to anticipate questions and answer them, and to anticipate problems and suggest ways to solve, mitigate, or avoid them. Frequent corporate updates on project progress are sent out to all participants in all locations.

Reward and Recognition

Within the context of change management, reward and recognition are given to those who exhibit desirable behaviors, provide feedback into the change process, and achieve high levels of performance with regard to the changed activities and/or processes. In the context of an ERP implementation, many companies have a clearly communicated incentive plan, which frequently expires after the go-live period. The change management team exists only for the implementation period. When the team disbands, the incentive plan disappears.

WHY CHANGE MANAGEMENT IS CHANGING

In the world of enterprise portals and workplace technology, change management is evolving from a project-specific into a holistic orientation. Three factors are bringing about this change:

1. A new generation of system users
2. The constant nature of change
3. The need for bottom-up as well as top-down change.

Digital Generation

Today's workers are living in a world where available information doubles in less than a year. For members of the digital generation (which consists of those who are comfortable with technology), job and employment cycles are shorter and faster. In fifty years the model has changed to one where jobs and roles were relatively static, to one where they are more dynamic. This generation is comfortable with learning and quickly adapts to new ways of working. In addition, they are used to living and working in an environment where knowledge transfer is not only top-down, but bottom-up and horizontal as well. The digital generation of workers is the first to come to the workforce with strongly developed technology skills. The learning media from 1960 to 1980 consisted of books, television, videos, microfiche, and classrooms. The learning media from 1980 onward consists of PCs, computer-based training (CBT), Internet, as well as books, classrooms, and video. Many of the digital generation have been using computers for a long time and live in homes in which PCs are as common as television sets or telephones.

Also, an increasing number of standards are in place across information technology systems. Many of those who use any system have been through more than one system implementation or have learned multiple systems. Moreover, those who have highly developed PC skills can move intuitively from one system to another. They have a better grasp of the standards that all systems share and of how to work their way through learning the particulars of a new system. They also have a better understanding of the change process and of how to change business processes quickly and efficiently.

For this generation of systems users, a technical system change does not have the heavy impact it once had. Among them, the fear factor accompanying a system change is not as large as it was in the 1980s or the 1990s. Additionally, people today are less apprehensive than in the past about creating either paper-based or system "work around" solutions. Companies have to be careful to keep up with employees' speed of change or suffer the consequences of disparate solutions that rely heavily on non-integrated systems and on each individual's idiosyncratic method for completing tasks within processes. Since people do not generally document their unique workarounds, when they leave the organization, their workarounds leave with them.

In fact, more individuals are flipping fear on its head and looking at technological change and new system implementations as an opportunity rather than a burden. Many individuals in every organization can easily see the business and personal benefits inherent in new technologies. They understand that learning to use a new technology increases their employability, both inside the company and on the open market. To these employees, change no longer means tediously adjusting to a new system. Rather, they see change as an opportunity to learn a new set of skills.

This new generation of IT systems users is even less suited to instructor-led training than the past generation. Step-by-step, rote training methods are not appropriate for people who from an early age have been teaching themselves how to use computer applications. Companies, therefore, must concentrate on offering training that provides different methods of learning: instructor-led where necessary (typically to introduce complex processes to large groups); expert-led (process training to small groups); and technology-driven (system training, simple transactional and process-based information).

For training programs to be successful with this new generation, they must have five distinct qualities.

1. They must be self-paced.
2. They must enable individuals to isolate and extract important information and to pass over information they already know.
3. They must be flexible, that is, able to add new, relevant material when necessary and appropriate.
4. They must include forums that enable learners to question experts directly.
5. Their focus must be on process and system intricacies rather than on navigation.

The workplace presents an environment within which constant knowledge transfer that has all of these desired qualities can be designed and presented to individuals who need it.

Constant Change

Change today is rarely a one-time event. It is constant and continuous. In such an environment, high-cost change management activities are no longer feasible.

Since change is constant, organizations should create an environment in which a constant flow of change-related information occurs. The focus of a change-management effort should no longer be the outcome of the change—moving from A to B, from "as is" to "to be". Instead, change should be seen as a permanent characteristic of the corporate environment, and a company's ability to handle constant change as a significant corporate asset. In fact, striving to achieve a specific "to be" environment is pointless. Today, as soon as a company reaches a "to be" goal, another one appears on the horizon. This is especially true in the complex, fast-changing inter-enterprise world.

Looking at this kind of environment through the prism of the old change-management paradigm can be stressful. If change is so emotionally draining, never being able to get off the change roller coaster can bring people to the breaking point. A new perspective is necessary, one that looks at business and change as a single-cell organism moving toward a stimulus such as food or light (in the business world, opportunity). With such a perspective, it is possible to understand how individuals must move, shift, change, and adjust, all very quickly, as the enterprise approaches the next stimulus that appears.

Top-Down and Bottom-Up Change

The top-down model of change management no longer works. In the new economy, executives and managers need to change behavior as much as those who work at other levels of the organization. They must entrust other employees to change and to manage their own change. They must reward innovation at all organizational levels and eliminate rigid hierarchies.

Because information flows faster than ever before, corporate leaders must reject the notion that knowledge is power and the hoarding of information that results from it. For companies to achieve the best results, they must disseminate strategic information to more people than ever before. Corporate cultures must move to a knowledge-sharing paradigm in which the ability to disseminate knowledge accurately and rapidly throughout the company is, in fact, the clearest sign of expertise.

In a world of instant-communication technologies, management communication must be frequent, to-the-point, and reliable. Facilitated by advanced communication devices and tight global networks, information often travels faster "through the grapevine" than it does through management messages. Add to this the fact that a dispersed, mobile, workforce often feels isolated and uneasy and that their lack of proximity to management puts them "out of the loop" about important corporate change. If management disseminates unreliable information, it will find itself in a losing battle with the company rumor mill.

The flip side of this information flow is the bottom-up communication that originates with employees. This communication is necessary both to give a voice to employees, who are potentially huge contributors to corporate knowledge, and to ensure that management gets a complete picture of activities going on throughout the entire company. Since accountability has been pushed down to employees who actually use the system, communication about their activities is integral to leadership's decision making. This is particularly significant for employees who are process owners, as well as for those who have client- or customer-facing roles and who can make the customer's voice heard throughout the organization.

THE WORKPLACE AS A CHANGE MANAGEMENT ENABLER

While the workplace is creating the need for a new change-management philosophy, it is also becoming one of the main tools of change management. This is true for a number of reasons:

- With the workplace, learning is dynamic. Working individuals learn to function in a constantly changing environment, rather than to use a particular system. People are also learning how to use the workplace tools to change their own work environment in ways that assist the company in its pursuit of business opportunity.

- The workplace allows central access to a pool of global knowledge, both within the corporation and across corporate boundaries with collaborators. Management communications, including communication about changes within the company and within the industry, can be pushed through the workplace.

- In this environment, the workplace is not just a link to all corporate systems, but to all corporate information. The workplace captures the knowledge, process flows, and tools inherent in a particular role. It also provides a familiar environment in which individuals at all levels of the organization can communicate about and act upon change.

- The workplace can also be a tool for rolling out a changed business process. A company can use the workplace to deliver the system changes created by the process change—accompanied by an explanation of the change, action items, and system instructions—directly to affected parties. Before the workplace, the ability to tie together process changes, system changes, and information about those changes did not exist, and the potential of this capability is huge.

NEW FACE OF CHANGE

Change today is very fast, very complex, and asynchronous. Each individual, defined by a role or set of roles, is affected by change in different ways. Some people's roles change more slowly, others' more rapidly.

Figure 9.2 illustrates very simply how, in the traditional model of change, everyone in an organization walked through change together. In the new change model, each individual role changes individually, and the steps that implement change for some roles are different from those for others.

Figure 9.2   New Complexity and Persistence of Change

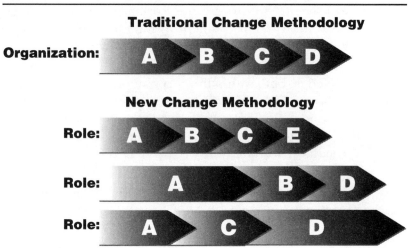

An optimal change management program today consists of three components:

1. Organizational change
2. Learning
3. Communication.

Organizational Change

The organizational design required in the old change management model has certainly not disappeared. Change still requires that resources be matched to business objectives and tasks. However, the workplace offers new tools and opportunities for implementing change.

An organization that defines its systems by the roles of the people who use them can drive organizational change through workplace implementation. The workplace not only delivers best practices (as ERP systems do); it also provides an understanding of roles and the organizational responsibilities that go along with them (as ERP systems do not).

A role exists to accomplish a business objective and is supported by the systems in place to manage processes. Corporate strategy must be designed to deliver the proper resources to the proper roles in order to accomplish the business objectives. Within their roles, individuals have the ability to change their workplace in ways appropriate to their daily tasks. Rather than completing a series of process steps, individuals are encouraged to utilize the workplace to its fullest potential to gain maximum benefit from the applications, information, and services available to help them accomplish the business objectives assigned to their roles.

Learning

In the new economy and the world of workplaces, specific training is only a small component of a much larger concept of learning. In this environment, employees are made aware that learning is a life-long process, not a series of discrete training exercises designed to teach individuals how to utilize a particular tool, system, or application.

Most employees—either those who have been through PC and system training before or those who are coming into the workforce fully equipped with PC skills—do not need training in the basic concepts of moving from paper to PC. Processes are still taught, but they are presented within a larger context and perspective. Processes are part of knowledge, experience, and relationships. Training increasingly is focused on how to acquire and share knowledge and on how to share experience and manage relationships.

Within a workplace environment, learning ERP navigation, for example, is much simpler than in the past, since navigating the Web-based workplace front end is much more intuitive than navigating static ERP screens. This reduces the need for step-by-step navigational training. On the workplace, information and documentation regarding implementation is much more closely tied to training, since both implementation and training focus on a role. Therefore, implementation documentation can be leveraged to reduce the development time for training materials. Curriculum can be closely matched to roles directly in the workplace, and each individual can maintain an ongoing record of his or her individual training plan.

As we noted earlier, the learning needs of individuals are best met by a combination of classroom- and technology-based training. In addition, the costs of training for specific tasks and the loss of work time to classroom time are both reduced after Web-based, self-paced learning is introduced. The workplace can then be used as a vehicle for deploying Web-based training, distance learning via the Internet, or an electronic performance-support system (EPSS). In effect, each workplace can be tailored to be a learning portal for the role. Such a learning portal can provide Web-based, self-paced learning, white papers, company policies and procedures, and quick lessons.

In the new economy, learning and training must be long-term investments; teaching people to be learners on their own is as important as teaching them to use a particular system. Learning opportunities must go beyond mandatory programs designed to teach explicit job skills and embrace the full potential of learning a myriad of new skills that are of interest to each employee.

Communication

Any employee communication program must be effective for the company's life span, not just for the duration of a change event. Companies will no longer be investing in communication programs for single projects; rather, they will invest in continuous communication mechanisms. The workplace is an effective tool that allows a constant flow of information from those who know about any particular issue to those who need to know.

Effective communication requires collaboration between management and employees. In a constantly changing environment, every individual is responsible for communicating change on a long-term basis. Employees must get this message loud and clear in a way that is acceptable to them. Management must also create a process throughout the company for proposing, approving, acting upon, and communicating change. With a Web-based front end, a company can use the workplace as a very effective tool for accomplishing these communication objectives. Through the workplace, messages designed to help raise acceptance of organizational change can be quickly and efficiently pushed to users, who, in turn, can provide feedback with equal speed and efficiency.

Unlike an ERP implementation, the workplace can be available for use as a communication mechanism even before it is configured as the access point to corporate systems. In this scenario, communication via the workplace can actually accustom those who will use it when it is fully operational to the system's attributes, while also providing people the essential change messages they need during the implementation of new technology.

KNOWLEDGE MANAGEMENT

In the late 1990s, the concept of knowledge management exploded onto the corporate scene. The term was used both to describe simple document management systems and to characterize an ideal knowledge-sharing environment—that is, one in which the correct information would be effortlessly accessible to the appropriate individuals and one in which all corporate knowledge (from process information to tips passed around the water cooler) would be captured and available in an organized and intuitive manner.

An enhanced ability to gather data creates a demand for more and better information. Updates on the progress of change or of any corporate effort—either discrete projects or ongoing accomplishment of business objectives—must be generated more frequently to satisfy the newly empowered user's desire for quality information. To match the needs of this environment, a knowledge management tool is required to capture and deploy the constantly growing and changing body of knowledge the corporation possesses.

In this book, we use the term *knowledge management* in a very practical way. A company must harness its employees' knowledge in order to create shareholder value. Information must be effortlessly exchangeable. Simply installing a computer system will not create such an environment. The best knowledge management is not solely characterized by artificial-intelligence tools that ferret out essential information. Rather, the best knowledge management programs are based on a set of flexible communication tools that enable individuals who have knowledge to identify other individuals who need it and to get it to them. As Figure 9.3 illustrates, knowledge management requires implementation both of tools and of organizational change.

The workplace combines rapid communication, collaboration tools, and access to information, applications, and services. This access is defined by roles rather than by position on an organizational chart. In short, the workplace provides a way for those who have knowledge to share it effectively with those who need it to fulfill their business objectives.

In order to establish a knowledge management system that the entire organization can use to communicate change, a company must simultaneously impose both a loose structure and stringent standards on the information that populates the system. In addition, corporate leaders must realize that one tool cannot be used to manage all knowledge; individuals must be encouraged to maintain a constant person-to-person exchange of information.

Figure 9.3   Components of Knowledge Management

A knowledge management system helps employees who are potentially impacted by any given change to identify the particular points that affect them. In a properly deployed knowledge management system, information flow follows process flow and is delivered according to roles. The workplace is not only the gateway to a knowledge management system, but the filter for it, ensuring that the right information is available to the right people at the right time.

On the organizational side of knowledge management, the filter concept must also extend to those who contribute to any knowledge management system. Contributors, knowledge workers, content editors, and others are able to push information through the workplace, but they must be responsible for constantly surveying available data, editing out duplication, and matching relevant information to roles.

A properly designed knowledge management tool achieves many-to-many rather than one-to-many (expert-to-users) communication. It consists of easy-to-use tools for adding new and for sorting out relevant information. It should be capable of managing different versions of information and of delivering it in different languages.

Knowledge management systems should be easy to navigate and organized, according to the company's structure, by information flow rather than by hierarchy. An individual using the knowledge management system should be able to get what he or she needs with a minimum of mouse clicks and in a way that is as personalized as possible. Careful consideration must be given to what type of information is important enough to push to individuals and to what type should be available for individuals to pull to themselves. Such consideration is essential if the knowledge management system is to be truly useful rather than merely chaotic.

A well-designed knowledge management system grows organically. That is, individual users, rather than system architects, build upon the system's contents. Subject matter experts should be responsible for their knowledge areas and act as content filters and editors.

Finally, knowledge is defined not only as explicit information about systems, processes, and business data, but also as corporate messages and missions. Figure 9.4 illustrates a knowledge

Figure 9.4   Explicit Knowledge Transfer

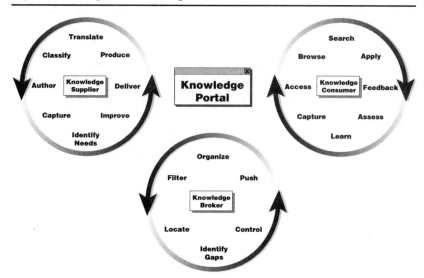

management system designed to integrate tightly with a knowledge portal (workplace).

RESOURCES REQUIRED FOR CHANGE MANAGEMENT

The way resources for change management are used today is much different than under the old paradigm. Today, to ensure that information flows and organization design (role definition) are consistent with corporate structure, the change management team consists of the entire staff of knowledge workers as well as system architects.

In addition, a knowledge management team needs to be in place to manage the system on an ongoing basis. Subject matter experts need to be in place to edit knowledge content, to audit, and to push the right information to the right people.

And finally, a human resources team must be responsible for linking appropriate reward and recognition to change. The team should continue on an ongoing basis. It is no longer sufficient that change management teams be staffed only for the duration of the implementation and that members then go back to their normal jobs after implementation is complete. As a process, change management should be embedded in the company's day-to-day operations.

What About Recognition?

In the world of the workplace, change is constant and intrinsic. Without the need for programmatic change, reward and recognition becomes more focused on meeting business objectives and less on behavioral change.

RISKS IN THE NEW CHANGE MANAGEMENT

There are a number of risks inherent in creating an environment in which constant and manageable change is the end goal. One involves the failure of senior management to accept and foster this new environment. Clearly, if senior management does not agree to accept a bottom-up, top-down, and horizontal information and authority flow model, such an environment cannot flourish. If management believes that moving to a workplace culture is simply another one-off change management effort, and if it fails to provide employees with a consistent and reliable stream of information regarding the effects and benefits of change, the initiative is doomed to failure. It will also fail if it lacks solid business processes for implementing change on an ongoing basis and if the knowledge management system is not dynamic and flexible enough to handle constant change information from a number of sources.

Human resources are affected by two major risks. First, individuals who for a long time have been in the same role, performing the same activities and tasks within the same processes, will not see the magnitude of the change the workplace can bring. Rather, they will view the workplace only as a new delivery mechanism. Second, this environment can, temporarily, create more work, longer hours, and higher stress levels, as people may be inundated with information and lose their ability to focus on the tasks and activities that previously defined their jobs.

Making change management work in a constantly changing world requires an understanding that no system can fix everything. Too often systems are put in place with unrealistic expectations. It also requires a realization that any system put in place will fail if it is not people-centric, backed by logical and efficient processes, and by communication of the reasons for implementation.

The role-based workplace is a more efficient and effective change communication tool than has ever before been developed. This tool, in combination with a solid and ongoing change management program that recognizes the needs and efforts of individuals who use the system, can be of great help to companies positioning themselves for success in today's new economy.

10

Implementing a Workplace and Driving Business Value

Moving from a systems/users model to a workplace/role model can drive a company's business value. Creating a dynamic workplace model positions a company both to utilize its current systems to their fullest and to create new e-style business models focusing on collaboration. It also allows corporate leadership to define a vision of the company and to focus clearly on the opportunities and challenges that come with achieving it. Corporate leadership, however, must analyze or determine these opportunities and challenges from both a top-down and a bottom-up perspective.

The top-down view concerns strategic imperatives of the new (networked) economy; the bottom-up evaluation involves cost reduction and efficiency-improvement issues. Any consideration of the company's future must include both as equal parts of the same equation.

Utilizing both the total cost of ownership and total benefit of ownership concepts (see Chapter 3), corporate leadership can determine how to derive the most value from the company's entire ecosystem: both the internal elements over which management has a great deal of control (e.g., managing costs), and external elements over which it has little control but that management can affect by aggressively pursuing an effective strategy.

One of e-business's greatest benefits—and also its greatest threat to established businesses—is that it affords new companies a chance to maneuver themselves into key positions in the value chain, disintermediating those around them. It also allows both new and established companies to cannibalize the value chain up or down from their original position. By defining individuals according to their roles in the company and by enabling access to all of the information, applications, and services they need to do their jobs more effectively, workplace technology fosters both the nimbleness and flexibility companies need to recognize opportunities to disintermediate others, and to respond to disintermedation threats from competitors.

Any public company's primary objective is to increase shareholder value. Accomplishing this objective requires that the company take into account the needs of other stakeholders—employees, customers, business partners and suppliers, and even the communities in which the company operates. Satisfying key stakeholders and, thus, achieving value for shareholders, is not solely the responsibility of corporate leadership. While corporate leadership is responsible for creating strategy and for planning macro tactics, employees at all levels of the organization can have an impact on the three ways value is created: growing revenue, lowering or avoiding expenses, and reducing the need for and cost of capital. Implementing a workplace-based information technology (IT) model can enhance both leadership's ability to set and communicate strategic direction and the ability of individuals throughout the company to act on that strategic direction to enhance shareholder value.

A successful workplace can unlock the potential of the Internet as a medium for collaborative business. The transition from intra-company integration to integrated inter-company business networks is the goal. Workplaces provide one of the means to achieve it.

HOW THE WORKPLACE HELPS
CORPORATE LEADERSHIP

Each member of a company's leadership team—the chief executive officer (CEO), chief operating officer (COO), chief financial officer (CFO), and chief information officer (CIO)—brings a different perspective to using the workplace to drive business value.

Among the CEO's major strategic concerns is looking for new business opportunities. However, he or she also must spend some time thinking about how to increase revenue from current operations and reduce or avoid cost, how to measure economic return, how to create a reasonable total cost of ownership, and how to determine the total benefit of ownership. Some research indicates that in many companies, all of the shareholder value is created by less than half of the company's capital and activities. The CEO is responsible for monitoring and maximizing those activities that lead directly to increased shareholder value and for eliminating or reorganizing non-profitable business lines.

Workplace technology, especially the push technology embedded in the workplace, provides the CEO with the key performance indicators he or she needs to make business decisions. It allows the CEO to disseminate critical strategic directives to employees as needed. The role-based nature of a workplace increases workflow throughout the company. The workplace also creates a flexible technical infrastructure through which the company can implement CEO directives more quickly and fluidly. Finally, the workplace's personal views increase customer retention, a major cost-saving objective.

The COO's key responsibilities include leadership in the areas of supply-chain management, vendor and supplier relationships, operational efficiency, effectiveness, and quality; and regulatory compliance. COOs use the workplace to streamline business processes and enhance workflow. Push technologies optimize interdepartmental communications and the tracking of key performance indicators. A workplace personalized around roles also ensures that each individual role receives the critical information necessary to focus properly on performance. By reducing the friction between suppliers and the company, and by alerting applicable areas of responsibility of possible errors, the workplace also allows the COO to monitor more closely and to speed up activities along the supply chain.

The CFO's primary concerns are overseeing regulatory financial reporting compliance and internal audit; providing business analysis to other corporate and, possibly, strategic business unit (SBU) leaders; improving the efficiency and effectiveness of the finance and accounting activities; and increasing profitability.

Using the workplace's push technology, the CFO can more easily streamline interdepartmental communications, track key performance indicators, monitor financial data within the company's data warehouse in order to alert appropriate parties to unforeseen financial circumstances, and keep abreast of shareholder value information and financial market perceptions concerning the company and its competitors. Finally, roles can be built to help facilitate internal audit processes.

The CIO's key responsibilities are to maintain the company's information and data integrity, manage information-service activities, and define and manage all computer and communication architecture and activities. The CIO must balance technological and operational needs with financial and marketing needs. He or she is responsible for seamless integration of data and information throughout the company's ecosystem.

Using a workplace, the CIO has central access to critical knowledge management activities. At the presentation level, the workplace cost effectively provides seamless integration of disparate systems. And because each individual has access to multiple internal corporate systems through a Web browser, the workplace reduces the risks inherent in traditional new system "roll-outs." With fewer applications on each "client" or desktop unit, less PC support is needed, freeing up IT staff to focus on making more applications, services, and information available through the network. Single sign-on and the transparency of the systems in the workplace environment also help reduce the burden on IT staff, who must be responsive to the specific systems or applications needs of the business units.

HOW THE WORKPLACE HELPS INDIVIDUALS

Each individual within a company should ask two questions about how he or she executes tasks and carries out work activities:

1. How do I/can I increase value for the company?
2. How can my relationships with customers, suppliers, or other business partners increase value for the company?

While corporate leadership creates company strategy, individual employees convert that strategy into shareholder value by the way they interact with the other players in the corporate ecosystem. Figure 10.1 illustrates the basic corporate ecosystem. Business value is generated at the intersections of the company and all participants in the corporate ecosystem.

While the workplace enhances each participant's ability to generate value for the company at the center of the ecosystem, it must also generate value for each participating entity. If only the central company wins, the relationships with participants will deteriorate, and eventually those participants will fall away. The cost of developing new relationships is much greater than the cost of maintaining relationships with existing participants. All relationships within the ecosystem must be win-win.

Figure 10.1   Company's Ecosystem

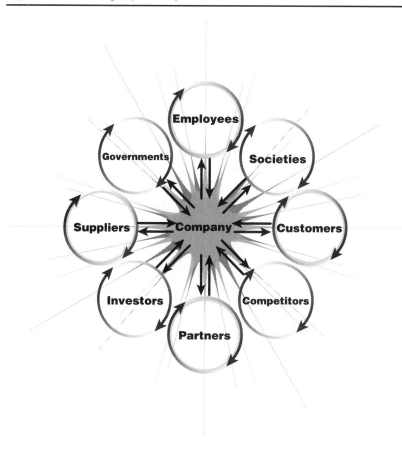

Roadblocks to achieving value exist at major intersections with collaborators: employees, suppliers, customers, and partners. At the company/employee intersection, the roadblocks are productivity, information access, awareness of individual importance to the big strategic picture, and cross-team/cross-department workflow and communication difficulties. At the company/supplier intersection, communications and logistics are the biggest roadblocks. At the company/customer intersection, they are communication, cost, relationship loyalty, and logistics. At the company/collaborative partner intersection, roadblocks include communication and logistics. When companies become more tightly linked in a collaborative web, an increased potential for roadblocks exists. The push technology enables control of the workflow and documention of all participant activities. As Figure 10.2 illustrates, workplace technology can help remove many of these roadblocks.

The workplace helps *employees* generate business value by delivering timely and cost-efficient access to high-quality information, relieving employees of cumbersome search and consolidation activities, improving motivation through ease of learning and use, and providing employees with the flexibility to enhance the way they perform their work. Employees derive value from self-service applications within the workplace.

The workplace helps *suppliers* generate business value by enhancing the company's buying power, increasing reliability and flexibility and decreasing cost of the company's inbound logistics, enhancing communication and coordination of supplier/company processes, and improving speed and convenience while reducing the cost of moving and processing transactions. Web access through the workplace makes it easier for companies to select a supplier. However, suppliers also benefit. Using the workplace as a Web entry point, they can reach a large group of potential customers without having to increase the size of their sales force. Lastly, the technology integrated on the workplace (supply-chain management and advanced planning and optimization for supply-chain goods, business-to-business procurement for MRO goods and repetitive-purchase production items) enhances business value by reducing suppliers' process administration costs.

For *customers*, the workplace provides business value by facilitating communication and process coordination, increasing speed

Figure 10.2   Using the Workplace To Open Roadblocks

and convenience while decreasing the cost of moving and processing transactions, improving customer retention and loyalty (through ease of learning and use), streamlining the buying experience and enhancing after-sales service, and growing the customer base.

For other *business partners* (banks, insurance companies, logistics providers, etc.), the workplace provides business value by driving down costs through access to common suppliers who are marketplace participants; allowing more real-time collaboration; and providing the best medium for sharing complex documentation, collaborating with former competitors, and generating new products and services.

Partners can derive additional business value if the company with which they are partnering extends to them the ability to use the applications on the workplace server. In such a scenario, the company itself may become an application service provider (ASP) for its collaborating partners. The converse can also be true. A partner can serve as an ASP for the central company. In this case, the workplace facilitates rolling out this service to employees.

IMPLEMENTATION BEST PRACTICES

Actually implementing workplace technology is not unlike implementing any other major computer system. A major difference is that a workplace implementation puts in place a dynamic system that is able to change and grow along with the company. The key similarity is that if the technology, rather than the development of new or enhanced business models, is the driver, the project will surely fail.

To succeed, the workplace implementation must be carefully planned; the right people must be involved; and all must understand the implications for supporting operating units and the opportunities to enhance business value.

Implementation Steps

The following are the four steps required to implement any workplace technology:

1. Determine the best solution set based on the industry in which the company operates, including which core processes and which systems satisfy the company's requirements. Early wins are important. Start with those areas where success is easily attainable and gains are easily and quickly achieved. Subsequent efforts will involve additional risks and larger potential gains.
2. Map a solution set to a rollout methodology that allows for continued growth and refinement. A workplace implementation is not a one-time event (Figure 10.3). Rather, it is the beginning of a continuous and user-transparent refinement of processes and systems (Figure 10.4).

Figure 10.3   Flat Development Cycle

Figure 10.4   Continuous Improvements and Refinement

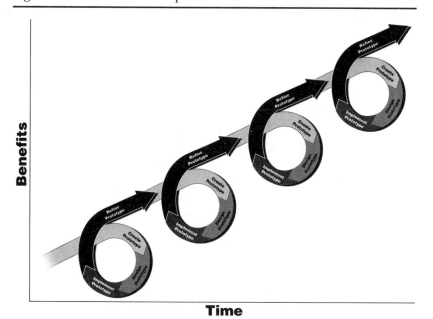

3. Map the solution set to the organization and the roles to the individuals.
4. Based on all of the previous work, configure internal data, systems, and processes to desired process modifications and to the new roles.

Five Keys to Successful Implementation

The five keys to a successful implementation are:

1. Measuring potential value
2. Aligning with business goals
3. Keeping the project focused
4. Holding beneficiaries accountable
5. Measuring success.

Measuring Potential Value

The potential value of a workplace begins with the business results corporate leadership wants to achieve. After identifying those results, management should map all the processes that need to be carried out in order to achieve them; determine, through benchmarking, the best-practice costs of those processes; and calculate the cost of producing quantifiable and measurable process improvements.

Aligning with Business Goals

Relationships are the key to achieving business goals. While enterprise resource planning (ERP) systems are about optimizing the information inside a company, e-business is about optimizing relationships among participants in the ecosystem. The workplace takes this e-business view as its starting point and then subsumes ERP. Workplace technology facilitates strong and trusting relationships among enterprise partners.

Keeping the Project Focused

The focus of any workplace implementation must be on information and flexibility. Unlike traditional IT systems, the workplace has no single, rigid, and inflexible configuration as its ultimate goal. The beauty of the workplace model is that it creates a flexible template that can change as change is required. In the workplace world, there is no big-bang go live that completes the implementation. Rather, as each new piece is ready, it becomes a viable part of the whole. If the workplace is to succeed, all levels of the corporate hierarchy must buy in to this new philosophy of systems implementation. Therefore, it must be constantly reaffirmed.

Holding Beneficiaries Accountable

In the workplace world, technology is more than ever an enabler, and individuals must be committed to taking advantage of its benefits. Because of this, individuals who will use the system must be involved from the beginning in planning how the implementation will occur. Even though a workplace implementation is gradual, it still involves a period of transition that employees must understand and for which they must be prepared. As well, individual departments or business units must forecast realistic benefits from workplace implementations and be held accountable for those benefits.

Measuring Success

With the workplace, implementation never ends. After the workplace has been installed, it is important continually to validate business results against stated targets. Once the workplace is up and running, management should continue to review the effort as the workplace evolves. This review should include monitoring projected benefits to ensure that budget goals are being met and refining the process to determine where additional benefits can be realized. Because the workplace is flexible and designed to accommodate "organic change," monitoring becomes, in effect, a way to determine the next gap between business goals and current capabilities and to plot the next steps in enhancing the technology.

Implementation Challenges to Members of the Ecosystem

All participants in the business ecosystem face challenges when implementing a workplace project. Challenges include involving *employees* and keeping them involved during the implementation, communicating the proper expectations for the workplace—both

CASE STUDY: ENABLING COLLABORATIVE BUSINESS IN THE AUTOMOTIVE INDUSTRY— A GLOBAL NETWORK OF SPECIALISTS

Figure 10.5 illustrates the process for developing, producing, selling, and servicing a new car. The car manufacturer sits at the hub of this network. This case study explains how utilizing workplace technology increases efficiency and effectiveness throughout the process.

On the development side, delivery times of assemblies and sub-assemblies can be cut by **up to 50 percent*** in some cases by as much as two months. A cost advantage of **up to $250 per vehicle** accrues to the supplier because of on-line sales, and the manufacturer can realize savings of **as much as 14 percent** on supply-chain costs.

Other improvements include reduced inventories throughout the supply chain, improved market intelligence and information about customer requirements and preferences, and faster reaction to market trends. Finally, with co-operative planning, quality and security increase.

On the distribution side, consumers engaging in on-line sales save **about $800 per vehicle**, and dealers reduce the amount of time a vehicle remains in inventory **by 40 days**, from 75 to 35.

Using online self-service, customers speed up their transaction time by **over 27 percent**. They are also able to configure the specifics of the car they wish to buy in terms of color and accessories. Communicating to customers online reduces **by more than 7 percent** the time it takes to provide them with important information; and the visibility of order-tracking information reduces the cost of sales **by another 12.6 percent**. Customers also receive their vehicles more quickly. All of this leads to dramatic increases in customer satisfaction.

*The business values quoted here are reported anecdotally by SAP customers or independent third parties. They do not represent industry averages.

Figure 10.5   Performing and Validating the Calculation for Proposed Business Value

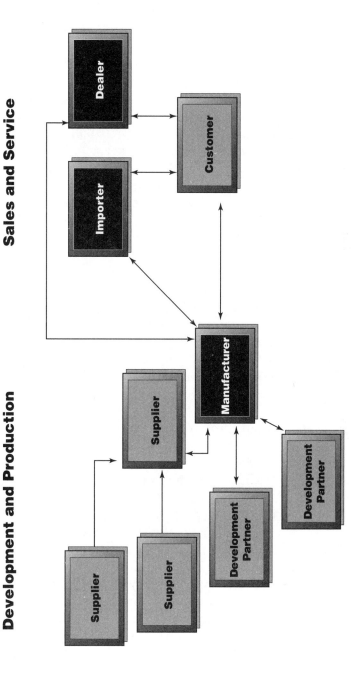

185

with respect to the implementation period and later when they must do business in the workplace environment—and convincing employees to accept and buy into the process of moving to a workplace environment.

Meeting these challenges requires that managers communicate expectations clearly, provide training and education, and promote the new way of doing business by involving people who actually do the work. In addition, a reward and recognition program that reinforces new behaviors is key.

Dealing with *suppliers'* challenges, such as changes to the business process flow, requires continuous communication throughout the implementation. To allay any fears, management might consider choosing one supplier with which to partner during the implementation period to test the system and increase roll-out support. Incentives also help to achieve supplier buy in. Finally, if possible, the company should partner with another of the supplier's customers to develop a standard approach to the new buying regime.

Customers and *collaboration partners* face the same challenges as suppliers. As with suppliers, it is helpful to partner with one customer and one collaborator during the implementation for testing and roll out support, to provide incentives to achieve buy in, and to partner with other businesses related to the customer and collaboration partner to develop a standard approach to new selling processes.

Collaboration partners face an additional challenge: they need to identify areas for convergence of business processes. To meet this last challenge, management must identify all potential collaborative partners and then produce a proof of concept for working together. The approach to collaboration must be carefully mapped out and the process prototyped on a small scale. The other ecosystem participants—governments, investors, competitors, and societies—face similar challenges.

As these challenges indicate, implementing and operating a workplace is not solely a technology issue. The more important issue involves strategic direction, that is, becoming a node in a networked economy as quickly and as efficiently as possible in order to improve business and, in many instances, to remain in business. Companies that fail to grapple with this issue do so at their own peril.

11

E-Business and the Workplace: A Broad View

In the world of e-business, physical matter is not important, and distance and time impose few constraints. Networks accelerate growth, and value rises exponentially with market share. Infomediaries have replaced intermediaries; buyers are gaining dramatic new power; and sellers are seizing new opportunities. Finally, business in the new economy is a one-on-one game.

Before concluding this book with our chapter on "Getting to Where You Want To Be," we thought it would be valuable to step back and take a broader look at the evolving e-business environment and at the technologies that have caused it to thrive, and then to set the workplace firmly within this "big picture" perspective.

B2B TAKES THE LEAD

In 1999, the financial markets were enamored of dot.com companies. Start-ups formed by a few recent business school graduates, whose only assets consisted of some used office furniture and a couple of high-speed computers, suddenly found themselves with market capitalizations larger than century-old industrial companies. This was especially true in the United States, where venture capitalists were falling over each other to see who could throw the most money at the newest dot.com.

Companies that sold merchandise to consumers—so called business-to-consumer or B2C companies—were the hottest. However, research consultancies that study such trends (e.g., Gartner-Group, Forrester, and Jupiter) accurately predicted that business-to-business or B2B transactions would quickly account for the vast majority of the monetary value of e-business. E-business has in fact increased opportunities among companies to use Web-based technology to buy and sell to and from each other. Why? The answer is simple. No matter how or when a consumer buys an item, that item has to be produced and delivered. If the item is a multi-component product, each of those components and sub-assemblies needs to be manufactured and then moved forward to the next step in the product's supply chain.

In addition, unlike B2B companies, B2C businesses—either start-up dot.coms or retailers trying to transform themselves into e-tailers—must spend millions of marketing dollars to get consumers to change their buying habits and buy over the Web. In the next few years, they may convince 20 or 30 percent of their customers to use this new channel. A manufacturer, however, can easily make it very attractive for its suppliers, logistics providers, and distributors to engage in transactions over the Web by establishing e-marketplaces that lower cost, streamline processes, and reduce cycle time. Because of the obvious and immediate advantages, buyers' and/or suppliers' acceptance of the Web as a business medium will be far more rapid than that of retail consumers.

OUT WITH THE OLD

E-business is forcing corporate executives to operate outside of their comfort zone. A company engaging in e-business is no longer defined solely by its product, history, industry, and relationship to its suppliers, competitors, and customers, who could be local, national, or global. Rather, it is defined by a new set of rules dictated by the evolving e-business environment.

As business processes and applications converge, competition increasingly comes from outside traditional industries or industry segments. For example, in some countries, energy is being deregulated and electric power companies are becoming both producers *and* transmitters of electricity. In addition, in this new business model, some transmission companies are redefining themselves as specialists in billing and customer relationship management for other companies. Some are supplying other sources of power such as oil and natural gas, and still others are supplying home appliances such as stoves and air conditioning units.

A generation or two ago, industry leaders could not even have imagined such transformations. Nor could they have envisioned the way products and services are presently being packaged and offered. Today's savvy corporate leaders, however, are embracing this vision to move their companies to the next level. They understand that those who do not continuously reinvent themselves are doomed to selling commodity products and services in a world increasingly dominated by ever-more finely tuned customer value propositions.

IN WITH THE NEW

In the past, success was largely based on the size of a company's investment, its location, its physical assets, or its history. Today, those criteria have been replaced by data, knowledge, and relationships. The current generation of successful companies is mining data and collating it into useful information and knowledge. Furthermore, these companies are using that knowledge to manage their relationships with suppliers, customers, and other business partners, seeking out new partners and finding new ways to work with old ones, moving from cooperation to collaboration, and using the right tools and skills to operate more efficiently and effectively. The end result is that customers are getting the highest value they have ever received, in the form of the best products and services.

E-Business Panorama: A 4-Box Model

The new world of e-business requires a holistic view or framework to help companies understand and implement the changes necessary to prosper at any given point in what we refer to as the e-business panorama (Figure 11.1). As our model illustrates, companies engaging in e-business use Web-based technology in one of four ways:

Figure 11.1   E-Business Panorama: A 4-Box Model

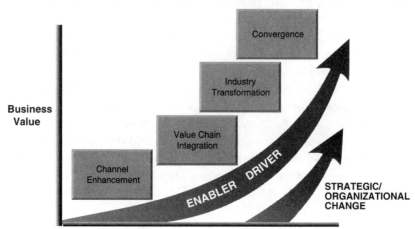

1. To create a new sales and marketing channel
2. To integrate the value chain, forging tight links with partners that move toward the creation of value networks
3. To transform industries by creating consortiums, marketplaces, and virtual organizations
4. To merge industries.

The e-business panorama offers a useful model that aids in understanding how these technologies can truly change the business environment:

- In the channel enhancement box, companies start using Web technologies to sell products and services and benefit by developing new skills.
- In the value-chain integration box, companies collaborate with some of their business partners on the Web having developed a level of proficiency with Web technologies that allows them to work differently. They benefit from cost savings and process efficiencies.
- In the industry transformation box, companies can create new business and organizational models because they

are working differently. They benefit from competitive advantage.

- In the convergence box, companies can respond differently to new or existing strategic opportunities because they have organized differently. They benefit from changes they drive within their own (and other) industries.

ERP AND E-BUSINESS SUPERCHARGE EACH OTHER

Web-based technologies are at the heart of the e-business revolution. But they are not the only issue that executives need to think about as they determine how best to allocate resources when implementing an e-business strategy. Because of the tremendous potential of Web-based technologies, many e-business evangelists are urging corporations to put their resources into expansion of e-business capabilities at the expense of investment in more traditional technologies, particularly enterprise resource planning (ERP) applications.

Nothing could be more wrong-headed. While e-business applications provide a company with the tools to communicate with employees and business partners, ERP applications provide it with the organization and consolidation of company data necessary to run the company at Internet speed. ERP tools provide consistent, reliable, timely, and accurate data about a company's internal operations and processes. They enable a company's current business processes to operate more efficiently and effectively. Without a handle on internal data, the flashiest Web site is merely a Web-façade, serving only to accentuate internal problems.

Once a company factors ERP into its e-business strategy, the e-business panorama 4-box model becomes considerably more complex, and more useful. We present this model (Figure 11.2) as a matrix that illustrates different degrees of internal systems integration on the vertical axis and the different boxes in the e-business model on the horizontal. We have added a "pre" step on the horizontal axis—no e-business capabilities—essentially as a starting point, either for a start-up company or for bricks-and-mortar companies that are still paralyzed by the possibilities of e-business.

Figure 11.2   E-Business/ERP Matrix

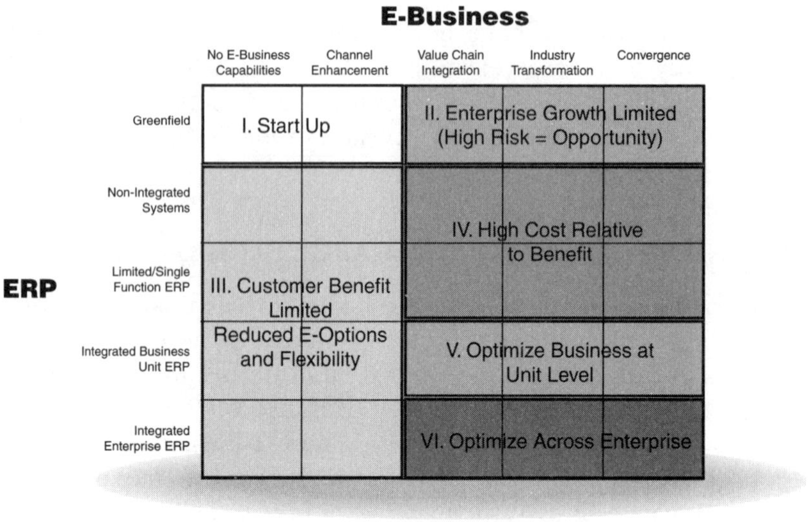

E-Business

ERP		No E-Business Capabilities	Channel Enhancement	Value Chain Integration	Industry Transformation	Convergence
	Greenfield	I. Start Up		II. Enterprise Growth Limited (High Risk = Opportunity)		
	Non-Integrated Systems			IV. High Cost Relative to Benefit		
	Limited/Single Function ERP	III. Customer Benefit Limited				
	Integrated Business Unit ERP	Reduced E-Options and Flexibility		V. Optimize Business at Unit Level		
	Integrated Enterprise ERP			VI. Optimize Across Enterprise		

The "spaces" a company can occupy across the ERP technology continuum are: greenfield, non-integrated systems, single-function ERP, integrated ERP in business units, or integrated ERP across the enterprise:

- From an IT perspective, a greenfield company is a blank slate. The company is new and has no information systems history. Because such a company lacks any legacy systems, it is free to develop a path to its desired e-business state unencumbered by its past IT decisions.
- A company with non-integrated systems has no rapid and meaningful data exchange among its internal systems that record business events. Such a company relies heavily on "black box" software and manual processes.
- A company with ERP by function has successfully installed one or a few major ERP modules (usually finance, human resources, and/or manufacturing) across all of its business units. But internal value chains in these companies still require manual intervention and management.

- A company with ERP by business unit has successfully installed a fully integrated ERP suite in one or more business units, increasing its ability to process the volume of customer and supplier transactions that come in through an e-business front end. This option is effective if the corporation operates as a holding company and as if each business unit has a separate value chain. If business units interact as each other's suppliers and/or customers, the situation is a less than ideal solution.

- Very few companies occupy the fully integrated ERP space. But those that do have a distinct advantage in implementing e-business solutions. They have the internal transaction engine in place needed to deliver on the promise of the company's Web pages, and the ability to show one face to the customer, not only in front-end Web page design, but also in the way the Web front-end interacts with the back-office processing activities.

We have grouped cells into six areas that share similar characteristics. Area I companies (start ups) are, generally, new companies having few systems. Companies in Area II have not invested in back-office technology and have thus limited their growth. Area III companies focus on back-office applications and, therefore, limit their options to capitalize on Internet technology to benefit themselves or their business partners. Area IV companies have attempted to exploit Internet technologies while not having upgraded their back offices and must spend heavily to meet the information needs of their business partners. Companies occupying areas V and VI have optimized their Internet and back-office systems at either the business unit or enterprise levels.

Migration Paths within the E-Business/ERP Matrix

The points of intersection between the e-business and ERP continuums form a matrix that presents a clear indication of where companies are in their overall e-business strategies and where they might aspire to be in the future. Figure 11.3 illustrates where most companies are today in the e-business/ERP matrix, and Figure 11.4 indicates where companies should aspire to be. Moving from

Figure 11.3   Where Most Companies Are Now

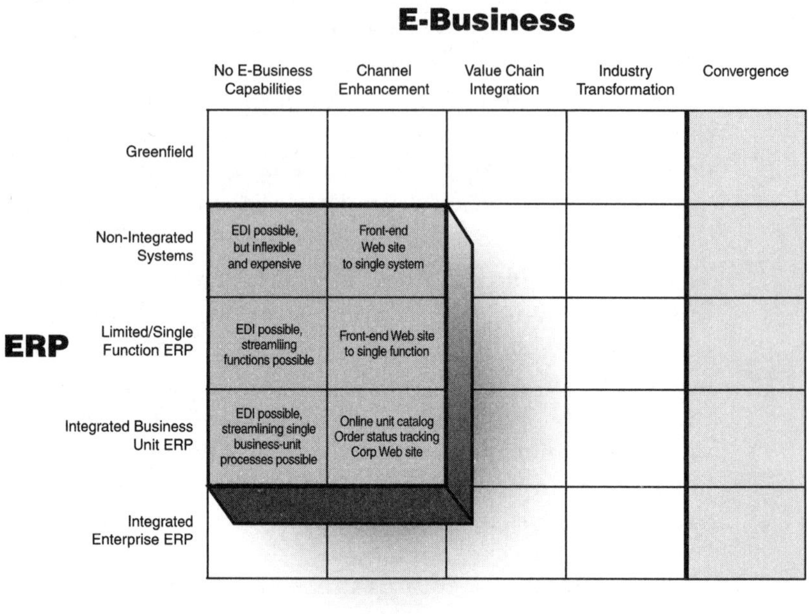

E-Business

	No E-Business Capabilities	Channel Enhancement	Value Chain Integration	Industry Transformation	Convergence
Greenfield					
Non-Integrated Systems	EDI possible, but inflexible and expensive	Front-end Web site to single system			
ERP Limited/Single Function ERP	EDI possible, streamlining functions possible	Front-end Web site to single function			
Integrated Business Unit ERP	EDI possible, streamlining single business-unit processes possible	Online unit catalog Order status tracking Corp Web site			
Integrated Enterprise ERP					

any starting place to any of the desired ending places, a company has a number of migration path options.

Getting from any starting point to any ending point is a four-step effort:

- Step 1 is determining the company's current position, based on its business strategies and its technology options.
- Step 2 is assessing the company's capabilities with regard to technology, processes, employees, and business partners.
- Step 3 is understanding that multiple migration-path options exist. For example, a company can choose to move horizontally and then vertically, concentrating on e-business strategies first and then focusing on getting its ERP systems up to optimal performance. Or it might choose to move vertically and then horizontally, putting the company's ERP house in order and then focusing on e-business. A third option is to move diagonally on the matrix,

Figure 11.4   Where Most Companies Are Headed

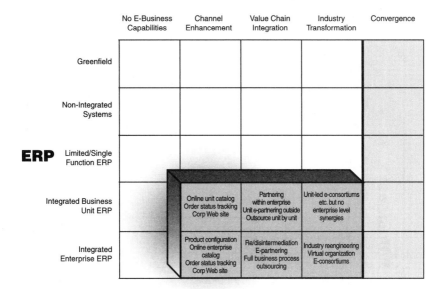

simultaneously putting resources into both ERP and Web-based technologies.

- Step 4 is choosing the best path—one that is realistic, clear, and manageable. This decision is based on an analysis of the technical feasibility of any migration path and of how well various migration path options meet the company's strategic intent and capitalize on its strengths. Also, company leadership must promote the chosen path, and staff at all levels must support it.

Figures 11.5 and 11.6 show the possibility of moving diagonally across the matrix, simultaneously improving the company's internal systems capabilities by utilizing ERP technology and improving the company's e-business capabilities. They also illustrate how different operating units within one company might be moving from the same starting point to different end points, or

Figure 11.5 Multiple Paths from Any Starting Point

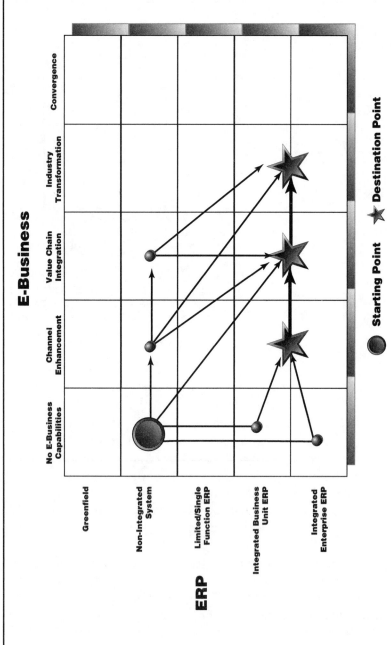

Figure 11.6 An Example of ERP Systems Migration in an E-Business Environment

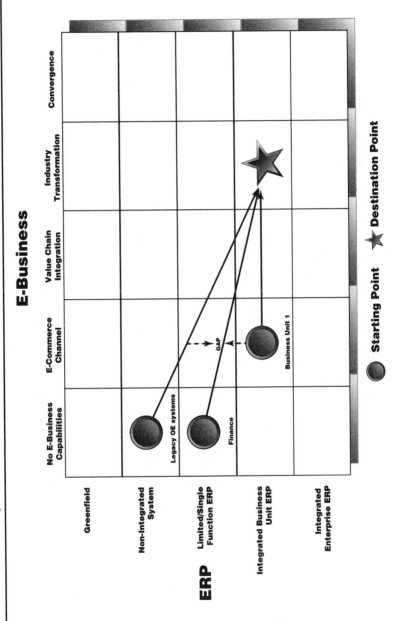

conversely, getting to the same end point from different starting points.

WHERE DOES THE WORKPLACE FIT IN?

While the changes we have described in this chapter are sweeping, companies that embrace workplace technology will have the edge in meeting the e-business challenge. Where does the workplace fit in this new environment? There is both a short and a long answer.

Short Answer

First, the short answer. From an e-business perspective, a company's employees can use the workplace to access various marketplaces quickly and efficiently. On the ERP side, a workplace allows a company to install, reinstall, or upgrade ERP systems at its own pace. By staying "behind" the workplace, the company can improve those pieces that are most critical to running its business in a way that is transparent to employees and other workplace users.

In addition, workplaces can be a great help to companies moving through the e-business panorama or choosing the best path option for migrating through the E-Business/ERP matrix.

Both the implementation of workplace technology on the enterprise level and participation in marketplaces on the inter-enterprise level become viable for companies in the second box of the four-box model presented earlier in this chapter, and almost imperative if they wish to move into the third box.

With respect to migration path options, portals provide points of entry to a collection of participating Web sites related by industry, services, functionality, or some other common ground. With workplace technology, a company can take advantage of a host of e-business opportunities without making a serious commitment to system ownership. Because the entire ERP suite does not have to be implemented at the company's site, the company can either "rent" ERP capabilities or implement those that are most utilized by the most important roles in the most important business processes.

The longer answer, however, involves a number of strategic considerations.

Long Answer: Four Strategic Options for E-Business

There are four strategic options for an existing company seeking to become an e-business. One is to integrate e-business throughout the company. A second is to find an e-business partner who can take the company's products and/or services and leverage them in an e-business model. A third is to spin off a separate e-business. And a fourth is to completely transform the company, rejecting the old physical model and recreating the enterprise as an e-business. Each of these models offers businesses opportunities in eight areas of competitive improvement:

1. Improved efficiency
2. Integrated processes
3. Reduced process costs
4. Extended reach
5. Reduced cycle time
6. Improved customer satisfaction
7. Reduced staff costs
8. Enhanced revenue.

Utilizing workplace technology, a business based on physical production of goods and provision of services can become an e-business in three-phases. In each phase, work needs to be done to develop the Web front end, enhance enterprise systems, and implement workplace components.

The first phase is building a solid foundation. In this phase, the workplace provides an opportunity for customers to configure product. It also provides the connections for single payment method, as well as lean manufacturing inside the company. Bar coding, labeling, quality tracking, shipment with third-party providers, and customer invoicing can all take place within the workplace. The process is completely transparent to the accounts receivable organization.

The second phase is improving the fit and finish. In this phase, the workplace provides multiple-ship-to-address and multiple-bill-to-address capabilities, as well as enhanced quality tracking, accounts receivable and accounts payable reconciliation, profitability by product, and supplier payment.

The third phase is achieving the long-term vision. In this phase, the workplace is used to integrate materials replenishment systems, perform all accounts payable, track vendor performance, and manage the relationship in vendor-managed inventory programs.

This is what makes the workplace unique. It is an advanced tool that helps companies accomplish concrete technology objectives, but is also integral to a company's e-business vision. In short, it is the first piece of technology that truly brings the pragmatic and the strategic under the same tent.

12

Getting to Where
You Want To Be

Companies around the world are just beginning to implement workplaces. In a 1999 survey of 100 mid-sized and large companies, *Computerworld* magazine found that while 28 percent had no plans to implement a workplace solution, 13 percent were in the planning stage, 16 percent had a workplace-type solution up and running in departments within the company, and 26 percent had a solution operating throughout the entire company.

A number of lessons have emerged from these early implementations. Not surprisingly, many of these lessons apply equally to other information technology (IT) implementation efforts, especially enterprise resource planning (ERP) systems.

The largest issues faced by most companies implementing enterprise portals have been security, traditional IT concerns about ownership of the project and the product, and business unit involvement in the system's design. Two issues specific to the development of workplaces also rank high among the concerns of companies involved in an implementation effort. One is their global reach and their need to secure both IT and business representation and support from global, geographic, and country organizations. The other is the fact that building a workplace is really an exercise in content development, as well as technology implementation.

From our experience and according to our research, the following are the four most important steps that companies building workplaces need to take:

1. Plan system security up front.
2. Prepare to spend more time dealing with content issues than traditional IT issues.
3. Involve all stakeholders at the beginning, so that different needs can be addressed in the workplace design.
4. Think big but start small.

IMPLEMENTING THE WORKPLACE

The workplace forces those in charge of implementation to focus on the human dimension of computer systems. It is designed to allow people to drive what the system does rather than to allow the system's constraints and logic to drive what people do. The workplace is intuitive and easy to navigate—attributes that should make a workplace implementation easier and more likely to succeed than other kinds of IT implementations. However, if the workplace is implemented through the prism of traditional system integration, that is, if the human component of the human/machine interaction is not given proper attention, the workplace will fail to deliver its full potential.

As Figure 12.1 illustrates, the timing of a workplace implementation differs from that of other system implementations. In a typical IT system implementation, project managers coordinate many disparate teams working on different aspects of the implementation. All aim toward one moment in time when the new system will go live. In a workplace implementation, the workplace shell can be installed immediately. Over time, the workplace can then be populated with various types of content.

Unlike an ERP system, which requires data transfers and configurations before it can be brought up and running, the workplace collects, collates, and delivers content from various systems. A workplace, therefore, can be introduced with very little true functionality. Figure 12.2 shows the vast number of different systems that many companies have installed over time. Many times

Figure 12.1 Pathway to Implementation

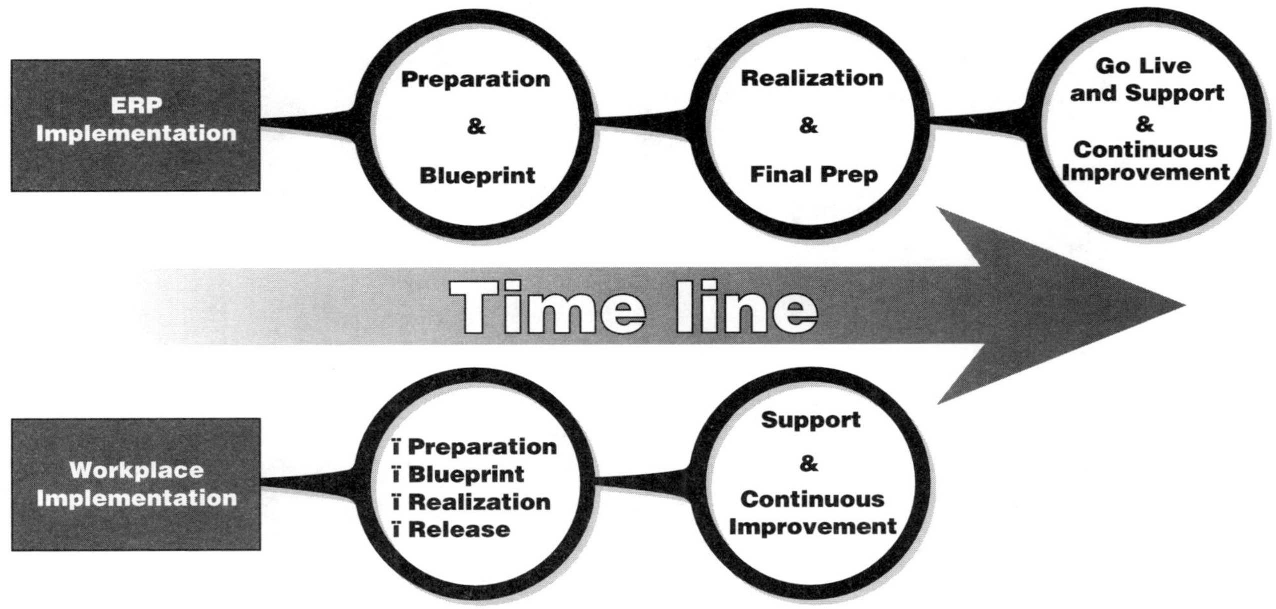

Figure 12.2 A Company's Systems in Chaos

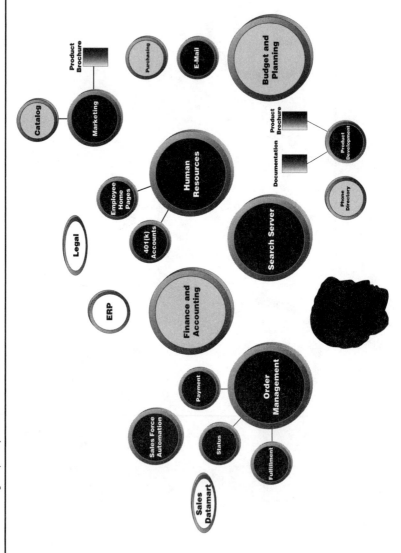

these systems have not connected with one another. Figure 12.3 illustrates how a workplace can be utilized to consolidate and organize these systems, and bring them through the workplace funnel in an organized fashion.

The speed at which workplace functionality expands depends on three factors:

1. The time it takes users to accept the workplace
2. The time it takes technically to bring discreet systems into the workplace
3. The time it takes experts to review and edit non-application content from both inside and outside the company.

CONTENT IS KING

Many companies are learning that getting a workplace up and running is easy. Continuously populating the workplace with useful content and information and providing additional useful

Figure 12.3   Workplace Technology Organizes a Company's Systems

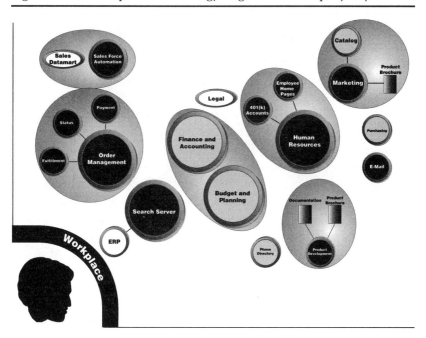

applications over time is far more difficult. The workplace has four purposes:

1. To link the company with its collaborators: customers, suppliers, and other business partners
2. To provide employees with easy access to outside research
3. To provide employees with a single window into the applications within the company's systems that they need to fulfill their roles in the organization's various business processes
4. To push timely information out to employees.

Developing this timely information is what many companies find most difficult about maintaining a workplace's usefulness. An important distinction exists between information and data. Merely pushing out data would not necessarily improve a working individual's productivity. Productivity is enhanced when intermediaries manipulate and analyze data, turning it into useful information.

Companies that implement a workplace must realize that they have, in effect, become publishers and assumed all the burdens of publishing. They include finding individuals who can provide content that is both attractive and intelligent and developing mechanisms to edit and fact check this content. This requires creating a mechanism that ensures content is not published before it has been reviewed for usefulness, readability, accuracy, and its legal implications and to make sure it does not adversely affect company relationships with collaborators.

Visits to clients who have installed mySAP Workplace bear this out: building such a content-development organization means that for every one technical specialist a company needs to maintain its workplace, it will require four-to-ten content specialists—researchers, writers, editors, and Web site and graphics producers —to provide a continuous stream of useful information to workplace users, depending on how extensive the portal's content offerings will be.

These content specialists must possess a journalist's rather than a software developer's or IT implementation professional's mindset. That is, they must be used to daily deadlines and capable of updating reports and quickly absorbing disparate facts. In addition to the content providers, companies need people to test, analyze, and determine the usefulness of new applications before they are added to those already available through the company's workplace.

DRAWING IN WORKPLACE USERS

The goal in a workplace implementation is to get the maximum number of people to use the workplace as quickly as possible. Accomplishing this requires populating the workplace early on with both highly functional as well as more "populist" applications and information. In Figure 12.4, a matrix illustrates where various applications and information fit in terms of number of users and importance. Across the two upper boxes, some applications are important for employees because they are highly functional and provide high corporate value; others are important because they

Figure 12.4 Content Balance Improves Workplace Acceptance

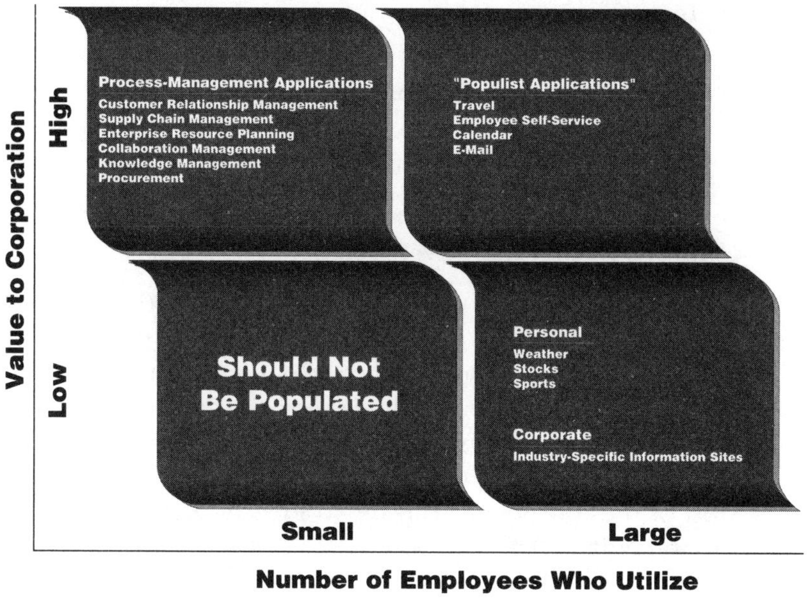

Value to Corporation

High

Process-Management Applications
Customer Relationship Management
Supply Chain Management
Enterprise Resource Planning
Collaboration Management
Knowledge Management
Procurement

"Populist Applications"
Travel
Employee Self-Service
Calendar
E-Mail

Low

Should Not Be Populated

Personal
Weather
Stocks
Sports

Corporate
Industry-Specific Information Sites

Small **Large**

Number of Employees Who Utilize

provide more personal value for individual employees in their roles. The lower left quadrant (small number of employees using an application with low value to the corporation) should not be populated.

A successful workplace roll out requires that employees have simultaneous access to applications that are useful to them (e.g., benefits management, critical reports, access to supplier records, and corporate travel management) as well as to process management applications that are more useful to the company (e.g., supply chain management or customer relationship management). Workplace designers must analyze the needs of individuals who will be using the system, and, based on that analysis, determine which products best satisfy both the company's and the individuals' personal needs as they fulfill their roles. This is an employee benefit that should be publicized early and often.

CRITICAL SUCCESS FACTORS

The success of a workplace implementation depends on five factors:

1. User-centered design and development
2. Inclusion of all relevant content
3. Control over the implementation
4. Funding for both the workplace and for knowledge management
5. Commitment to an infrastructure provider.

User-Centered Design and Development

To guarantee workplace success, designers must work collaboratively with those who use the workplace. While content is important, so is the method used to deliver it and the design of the content-delivery vehicle. If the delivery method is wrong, the message easily can be lost. Also, if the design of the content-delivery method is not attractive and user-friendly, the content itself may be ignored.

Most of these problems can be avoided by engaging professional usability labs that can be objective about user issues like workplace design and navigation. Designing for users is not a technical issue, nor is it accomplished by designing more features or functions. For usability designers, the most important issue is understanding the work processes of users and the business processes of an enterprise. In developing an approach, usability designers must:

- Observe users performing their tasks and activities
- Derive an understanding of users' primary goals
- Establish usability goals that the interface must achieve
- Design an interface that supports those goals
- Test the interface to determine if it meets the goals.

Once these broader objectives have been met, usability engineers or interface designers should then focus on the more traditional usability issues: meaningful icons, intuitive and understandable site navigation, meaningful field labels, relevant options, and powerful performance support tools. Also—and this is extremely important—users should be involved throughout the development process to test and validate design.

One important design issue involves presenting users with at least an approximation of a world they already understand—a world in which they do not need to be trained to live. Designers will frequently use graphical metaphors to construct this approximate world. For example, almost all shopping sites today incorporate a graphical shopping cart to approximate a real world shopping experience on the Web site. Users are familiar with how shopping carts are used: items are placed into or removed from carts and, when finished, shoppers empty the carts and pay.

Developers of successful sites have taken advantage of the shopping metaphor. Visitors to these sites need no training. Unsuccessful sites have blundered by altering the shopping process, for example, by requiring a shopper to "show" a credit card before selecting an item. (Who would ever pay for something without first looking at it?) Other sites told the user to "edit" a shopping cart. (When was the last time anyone "edited" a bag of carrots from his or her shopping cart?)

The basic point is this: getting the design right is an iterative process. Usability labs can surface the issues and identify the "sore thumbs" to ensure that the workplace is easy to use and that using it is an enjoyable experience.

Inclusion of All Relevant Content

In a workplace environment, the terms intranet and extranet are obsolete. Both individuals within the company and their collaboration partners outside the company use the same Web-based front end to access the host of information, applications, and services available on the workplace. Roles determine the particular information, applications, and services to which users have access.

A company must design its workplace with a clear understanding that partners who once used the company's extranet technology will now be using the workplace and that they will have access—depending on their roles—to the same information, applications, and services available to company employees.

The company has to decide how much content it wants to produce to push to users outside the company itself. Providing separate push content for customers, suppliers, and other business partners can become a very expensive proposition but can also add greatly to the workplace's value to these collaborators. As indicated in Chapter 6, strong content can create communities of users outside the company and can make the company's workplace the community of choice for collaborators seeking access to third-party services.

Control Over Implementation

Multiple levels of control must be imposed over implementation at the corporate, business unit (if applicable), and project levels. At the corporate level, the important elements to control are access, security, and overall look and feel of the workplace (or workplaces) being implemented. If business units will be implementing separate workplaces, a corporate level group should have input into design parameters and content categories. Collaborators who deal with more than one business unit and, therefore, who will utilize more than one workplace must be able to navigate easily and to depend on finding many similar features in each workplace.

At the business-unit level, opportunities should exist to personalize the workplace while still maintaining the corporate guidelines with regard to design and content. Different business units will need to focus on or highlight different elements of their business processes for their collaborators.

Throughout this effort, the fine line between structure and chaos must be maintained. Among the greatest virtues of workplaces are that they are flexible and able to accept personalization. Yet, a company needs to maintain its ability to present one face to the customer by ensuring that customers who deal with many different business units utilizing many different workplaces have a similar experience when using each. The level of flexibility in the implementation and design of business-unit workplaces will depend on the industry or industries in which the company works, as well as on corporate and business unit organizational cultures.

To guarantee success of the corporate workplace, senior IT management, including the CIO, should be involved in budgeting, procuring the system, and marketing the virtues of the workplace to employees and leaders across the business units and at the corporate level.

Funding for Both the Workplace and Knowledge Management

Ensuring that the workplace makes corporate content more valuable requires that it be tied very tightly to the company's other knowledge management efforts. A company should use some of the money budgeted to knowledge management projects to get its workplace up and running as quickly as possible and then to continue to populate it with the knowledge necessary for all of the people who use the workplace to do their jobs more effectively.

Commitment to an Infrastructure Provider

Basic infrastructure technologies, such as Web servers, databases, and directories, go in to the building of a workplace. Companies must align their investment in these technologies with their other client infrastructure commitments.

There is value in using a single vendor for infrastructure technologies. Using the same vendor:

- Cements the vendor relationship and increases the vendor's commitment to resolving technical integration issues
- Provides the company with a greater influence with the vendor by virtue of a higher dollar-volume of business
- Facilitates the integration of the complete technical solution. Using the same vendor makes the technical solution less complex, since data structures, taxonomy, and communication protocols already have been established
- Reduces the translation of data, thereby lowering the company's reliance on middleware for setting up, configuring, and maintaining data.

MITIGATING RISKS

Three techniques can be used to mitigate the risks inherent in implementing a workplace environment:

1. Design and implement in a modular fashion
2. Line up executive sponsorship
3. Design for early success.

Modular Design

Modular design easily accommodates continuous change. In order for a workplace to be continuously successful, those who manage it must never stop learning from those individuals who use it. Modular design allows the workplace to grow and change in an organic way, as business necessities change and as the way individuals utilize the workplace changes. A modular design allows a company to add new applications, information, and services to the workplace over time and to bring new individuals into the workplace as needed and as new roles are defined.

Modularity does not mean adding building blocks without a plan. In fact, successful modularity depends on complete and thorough planning right from the beginning. A homeowner does not erect a concrete wall if he or she plans to expand the garden the following year. One saves oneself the time and expense of drilling through concrete by planting a "green" wall or a wooden trellis that can be reused. Like the homeowner, the system builder must have a strategy and must engage in detailed planning to ensure that applications and infrastructure implemented today do not preclude future expansion. This is especially true in a system landscape that includes many different servers and networks that are geographically dispersed. Systems administration can also be distributed, but one person must be responsible for having the overall picture in mind. That person, often the global system administrator, uses the equivalent of a cockpit to maintain an overview of all the systems under his or her command. At a glance, the administrator can see where the problems are located and can drill down to obtain more details. The cockpit can also provide a graphical display of the systems landscape. Links to an automated maintenance application can ensure that service engineers, whether in-house or in the field, can quickly respond to and correct any problems. Such an application can also maintain statistics and report on problem areas.

Some sources report that networks will eventually represent 50 to 70 percent of the total costs of running a workplace. During the implementation, network costs are less than 10 percent. Equipment procurement and upgrades are the big cost factors during workplace implementations, often accounting for over 50 percent of the total costs. Figure 12.5 shows both the initial cost and operating cost for a workplace.

Figure 12.5   IT Costs of Workplace (Installed Base)

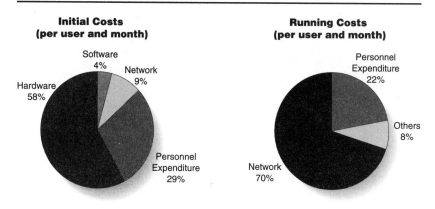

Source: SAP Internal Study

Executive Sponsorship

Executive sponsorship is a must. Moving to a workplace environment is possibly the most radical—and most necessary—change a
company will ever undergo. Business process reengineering,
shared services operations, and earlier IT systems implementations
have always been major efforts. However, companies moving to a
workplace environment will also be defining and designing new
business models. For the workplace to be successful, corporate
leadership may have to undergo more behavior change—in terms,
for example, of sharing knowledge and information and allowing
for bottom-up process redesign—than others in the company.

But executive sponsorship is not enough. All members of the
business ecosystem who use the workplace must be involved in its
design and continuous improvement. User-centered design invites
individuals not only to use the workplace but also to suggest ways
in which it can be modified to be even more useful.

Design for Early Success

Early wins are the key to any successful change implementation.
Early leadership support energizes those working in the implementation trenches and generates enough funding to move the effort forward on a "pay its own way" basis.

Those managing the workplace implementation must understand their own company well enough to know where those
early wins can occur. Designing a workplace implementation for
early success means spending time up front configuring, defining
roles, and determining in what order information, applications,
and services will be brought in to the workplace format. In all of
these activities, ease of use, navigation, and access should be para-
mount considerations.

WHO OWNS THE WORKPLACE?

Implementing a workplace involves a myriad of turf issues. While
workplace technology is inherently democratic, giving individuals
access to more applications, information, and services than ever

before, throwing open the gates could lead to a state of anarchy. Therefore, a company moving to a workplace environment needs to determine ownership on three different levels:

1. Who owns the implementation project?
2. Who owns the product, that is, the applications, tools, data, content, workflow, and business processes?
3. Who owns the infrastructure, that is, the hardware, software, networks, PCs, servers, and other devices?

In a typical ERP implementation, either the IT Department or a business area, like finance or human resources, owns the implementation. Information technology will often stress a "technical" solution that ignores human issues such as change management, knowledge transfer, and training. If a business area owns the implementation, the resulting "product" might not be technically feasible, either because it lacks an infrastructure completely or lacks one that can support it. In addition, the "product" might be too expensive to maintain or require expensive and/or exotic hardware and software in order to function.

Allowing an upper level management team to own the project may mean that others in the organization fail to take ownership. For example, one workplace project that was perceived to be the executive VP's baby completely lacked organizational support and died a slow, painful death, taking the IT team with it. Conversely, if the project is exclusively a "grassroots" effort, it may have the support of a large number of potential users but lack corporate sponsorship, the key to money and influence. Without these "accelerators," such projects go nowhere. The moral of the story is this: projects need buy-in and support from all levels—IT, business areas, upper level management, end users, training, and support. The levels of ownership change as the project evolves from implementation, to live, to continuous support.

Figure 12.6 illustrates which participants play roles in which aspects of workplace implementation during the design phase, during the release when the workplace is first being used, and during the refinement stage when it is being more fully populated with information, applications, and services.

Figure 12.6   Level of Involvement in Workplace Implementation

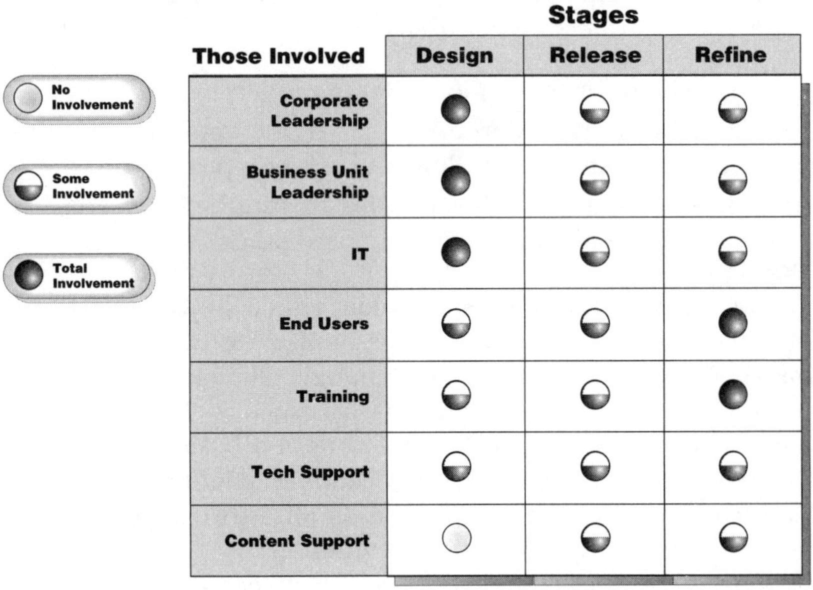

Legend	Those Involved	Stages		
		Design	Release	Refine
No Involvement (○)	Corporate Leadership	● (Total)	◒ (Some)	◒ (Some)
Some Involvement (◒)	Business Unit Leadership	● (Total)	◒ (Some)	◒ (Some)
Total Involvement (●)	IT	● (Total)	◒ (Some)	◒ (Some)
	End Users	◒ (Some)	◒ (Some)	● (Total)
	Training	◒ (Some)	◒ (Some)	● (Total)
	Tech Support	◒ (Some)	◒ (Some)	◒ (Some)
	Content Support	○ (No)	◒ (Some)	◒ (Some)

MANAGING EXPECTATIONS

Throughout this book we have stressed the importance of the working individuals who use the workplace to its ultimate success. Their expectations about this technology, therefore, are critical and must be managed very carefully.

Users should know from the outset that while the workplace is a flexible and interactive tool, it will not solve all of their problems or meet all of their challenges. For example, they may not be able to get all the information they need with one click. They will, however, be able to access much more information than they are used to getting without having to log on to many separate systems.

Management should be prepared to respond to the following unrealistic expectations:

- Everyone will embrace this change.
- Additional learning will no longer be necessary.
- All change will cease.

- The workplace will serve as a quick fix for bad processes. The workplace does not replace the shortcomings within any application or system.

- Roles are static. In fact, roles are highly dynamic. As individuals learn how to get more from and do more with the workplace, their roles can—and really must—change to incorporate those gains. At the same time, corporate leaders should not have unrealistic expectations about how much productivity will increase.

- There is a single point in time when the workplace will "go live" and the implementation will stop. In reality, because the workplace is an organic system, it will continue to change as a result of ongoing additions to and deletions from the array of applications, information, and services it incorporates. Because of this organic quality, calculating the payback period for a workplace implementation can be difficult. The project is ongoing and is always in a simultaneous payback and re-investment mode.

In our opinion, the best way to deal with unrealistic expectations is to stress through repeated communications the benefits that the workplace can actually deliver, such as ease of use, intuitive design, fast system response, and single password/single sign-on. Individuals should also assume that they will be able to use a workplace without having to take a training course first and expect that the workplace will make them more productive in a positive way. Moreover, the workplace is a tool to enhance work/life balance by making it easier for people to connect to important information, applications, and services from anywhere at any time. With the workplace, working individuals can expect to achieve an added flexibility in their work regimen.

When these realistic expectations are confirmed by management and, ultimately, by the technology itself, many of the change issues discussed earlier resolve themselves. Working individuals who know what to expect from the workplace—and what not to expect—are better prepared to use it to its fullest potential to enhance their working lives, while, at the same time, dramatically enhance the company's ability to meet its business objectives.

FINAL WORD: THE ENABLING
POWER OF THE WORKPLACE

Over the years, a great deal of money, time, and energy has been invested in improving the information people need to perform their jobs. Unlike previous solutions, the workplace provides a golden opportunity to deliver information that is *pertinent* to a working individual's role; *filtered*, eliminating the need for individuals to wade through so much information that they become frustrated by the process; and *flexible*, so that even when roles change, the system remains relevant, easily navigable, and useful. In short, by positioning working individuals to be truly informed by the information systems they use, the workplace makes work more interesting, productive, and satisfying. In doing so, the workplace takes a giant step towards fulfilling the ultimate promise of technology: to enhance the lives of the people who use it.

Glossary

Advanced Planning and Scheduling (APS): Sophisticated decision-support applications that use linear programming logic to identify optimal solutions to complex planning problems that are bound by material, labor, or capacity resource constraints.

Application Programming Interface (API): Calling conventions that define how a series is invoked through software. API allows programs written by users or third parties to communicate with certain vendor-supplier programs.

Application Service Provider (ASP): A company that offers software applications for "rent" over the Internet.

Authentication: The process of determining if someone or something is, in fact, who/what he/she/it purports to be.

Authentication of Receiver: Assurance of the receiver's identity.

Authentication of the Sender: Assurance of the sender's identity.

Confidentiality: A system by which only the sender and receiver can interpret document contents.

Customer Relationship Management (CRM): An integrated combination of software tools, business processes, and employee skills that allows a company to provide enhanced sales and service to customers, including personalized marketing, promotion, and pricing.

Digital Certificate: An electronic "credit card" that establishes an individual's credentials when doing business or performing other transactions over the Web. It is issued by a certification authority and contains the name, serial number, expiration date, and digital signature of the issuing authority and a copy of the certificate holder's public key. Some certificates conform to the standard X.509. Digital certificates can be kept in registries so authenticated users can look up other users' public keys.

Digital Signature: An electronic rather than written signature, which can be used to authenticate the identity of the sender of a message or of the signer of a document transmitted electronically. It can also be used to ensure that the original content of a message or document has not been changed.

Enterprise Resource Planning (ERP): The information pipeline system within a company that allows it to move internal information efficiently so that it may be used for decision support inside the company and communicated via the workplace to business partners throughout the value chain.

Firewall: A firewall protects a company's internal computer systems through dedicated hardware and software that screens network traffic and validates information flow between networks.

Integrity: Assurance that the message contents have not been altered.

Key: In cryptography, the key is a mathematical algorithm that is applied to the string or block of unencrypted text (a message or a digital signature) to produce encrypted text. The length of the key determines how difficult it will be to decrypt the message.

Non-repudiation: The parties to a transaction need to be certain that neither can repudiate an agreement once it is agreed to. Security technology can prevent a party from claiming he or she was not one of the signers of an agreement.

Non-repudiation of Origin: The sender cannot deny having sent the message.

Non-repudiation of Receipt: The receiver cannot deny having received the message.

Portal: A window into an integrated set of information, sometimes with software applications and services added. A portal can be established by a software vendor to Web-enable its set of applications, by an industry participant to join together suppliers and purchasers throughout the value chain, or by a third party in an effort to aggregate and intermediate purchasing and selling or to provide content to a particular community.

Private Key: In cryptography, a private or "secret" key is an encryption/decryption algorithm known only to the party or parties that exchange the message or digital signature.

Public Key: In cryptography, a public key is the algorithm provided by a designated authority that, when combined with the private key, can be used to encrypt /decrypt the message or digital signature.

Public Key Infrastructure (PKI): A group of individuals who receive a certificate that uses the same public key.

Role: An individual's role is defined by the set of activities and tasks the individual undertakes and the relationships the individual maintains in order to accomplish his or her work. An individual's role determines the information, applications, and services within the workplace to which the individual is allowed access. An individual may have many roles, some of which are temporary, such as project manager, or project team participant. Individuals outside the organization that implements the workplace can have roles based on the relationship to the organization that allows them to utilize the workplace.

Secure Socket Layer (SSL): The SSL protocol is the most popular way to protect sensitive information such as payment data. SSL encrypts data sent between two parties by constructing a communication connection in which all data is encrypted before being transmitted over the Internet. The handshake routine at the beginning of the SSL session shares the identities of the parties, selects one of several encryption algorithms that have been pre-designated for possible use, and creates the session-specific encryption keys.

Session: Pages/dialog steps that logically belong together to perform a certain task with a defined start and finish. A typical session on a Web application server involves a sequence of requests and responses unique to the session.

Single Sign-On: The ability to sign onto a workplace only once and receive access to all the systems one is authorized to use.

Supply Chain Management (SCM): The activities, tools, and software that allow a company to integrate production more tightly across business partners within a value chain. Supply chain management software includes sophisticated planning software such as APS.

Trust Center: A certification authority that signs digital certificates. Authentication based on digital certification is produced by the trust center.

Web Browser: Software that allows a user to view and interact with content on the Web or on a company's enterprise portal (workplace). The browser processes text, graphics, and in some cases, sound and video. It also downloads and processes files as required.

Web Server: The hardware and software that retrieve Web information and transfers Web pages to the Web browser.

Workplace: An enterprise portal that is designed to provide each individual access to particular information, applications, and services based on the role(s) that individual fulfills inside or outside of the organization that implements the workplace.

Workplace Builder: Design and programming tools that allow an organization to customize the front-end design of the workplace, as well as the way information, applications, and services are brought to the workplace front end.

Appendix

Using the CD-ROM

The CD-ROM included with this book contains a variety of information about mySAP Workplace and about enterprise portals and their benefits. It also contains SAP MiniApps that you can use in your own enterprise portal and mySAP Workplace demos. You can also use the CD-ROM to sample a live mySAP Workplace if you have Internet access.

SYSTEM REQUIREMENTS

To enhance your experience with the CD-ROM, make sure your computer meets the following recommended system requirements. If your computer does not meet these requirements, you may experience problems with some of the contents of the CD-ROM:

- A PC or laptop with a processing speed of at least 233 MHz
- A CD-ROM drive
- 64 MB RAM
- Graphic 1024 × 768
- Microsoft Windows 95/98/2000 or Windows NT 4.0
- Internet Explorer 4.0 or higher or Netscape 4.0 or higher
- Modem or network connection with a speed of at least 28,800 bps (if you intend to visit the mySAP Workplace or access the Web links)
- Internet account (if you intend to visit the mySAP Workplace or access the Web links).

CONTENTS OF THE CD-ROM

Customer Successes

We have included customer testimonials that describe how, using workplace technology, real companies achieved real benefits and efficiencies for themselves and their employees.

Demos of mySAP Workplace

We have created a number of sample portals for employees and external communities using workplace technology. Workplaces can be tailored and customized according to the needs of employees and their roles. As an example, run one of the screen cams for a sales representative or business analyst.

Test-Drive mySAP Workplace

You can also experience a real workplace by accessing SAP's Internet Demonstration and Evaluation System (IDES). This is a live system, access to which requires a network or modem connection. A user name and password will be provided.

MiniApps

MiniApps form the push portion of the workplace and deliver a variety of content to the user. They are the windows to underlying application and productivity tools and deliver information and services to the user in a simple way. We have provided examples of the latest MiniApps that you can download and have your system administrator install in a workplace.

Web Links

The CD-ROM contains links to sites that will give you more information about SAP, its subsidiaries, and its partners.

We welcome reader feedback about this book and CD-ROM. Contact us directly by choosing the *Contact Us* link on the CD-ROM home page.

Remember: To use these links, you must be connected to a network or have a modem connection.

Additional Information

We have also provided a number of fact sheets, white papers, and presentations that provide additional insight into enterprise portals. Download these documents to your computer, or print them to read later.

Additional Software

In addition, the following software is included to help you access the CD-ROM's various components:

- Adobe Acrobat Reader 4.0, to view and print documents
- Microsoft Internet Explorer 5, to view documents, portals, and mySAP Workplaces. (Note: This is the optimal browser for running this CD-ROM. However, the CD-ROM will also run on Netscape Navigator 4.0 or higher.)
- Macromedia Shockwave 8.0 Plugin, to view the portals and the mySAP Workplaces

HOW TO USE THE CD-ROM

Insert the CD-ROM into your computer's CD-ROM drive. The CD-ROM is self-starting. Within a few seconds, you will be welcomed to the CD-ROM's start page.

If you don't see the start page within a few seconds, the self-starting default has been turned off. If that's the case, go to the main directory of the CD-ROM and double-click on start.exe. This will take you to the start page on the CD-ROM.

PROBLEMS WITH THE CD-ROM?

Problems with the CD-ROM are most likely caused by insufficient memory (RAM) or by other programs running on your computer that affect the running of the CD-ROM and its programs. If you are experiencing problems, try disabling any antiviral software that you are running and closing all other running programs, thereby freeing up additional memory.

If you are experiencing difficulty when trying to access a Web link, make sure that you are connected to a network or that your modem is functioning properly.

The CD-ROM also includes a readme file with additional instructions. You may want to print the contents of this file and have hard copy available as you sample the CD-ROM's various features.

If, after taking the above steps, you still are having problems, send us an e-mail using the *Contact Us* link on the CD-ROM home page, or e-mail us at info@sap.com.

About the Authors

Thomas Anton, B.A., M.S., is an SAP AG product manager assigned to the mySAP Workplace. Based in Germany, he joined SAP in 1987 as a sales and distribution applications developer and has since held several other positions in the area of application development. In addition to the mySAP Workplace, Mr. Anton has participated in EnjoySAP and other SAP global initiatives focused on customer feedback.

Peter Barth, B.S., M.S., Ph.D., is the director of corporate marketing for SAP's mySAP Workplace and related technologies. Prior to joining SAP AG in Germany, he spent two years as a consultant helping clients to develop and implement successful IT strategies and advising them on operations issues. A computer scientist by training, Dr. Barth is also an expert in operations research.

Ian K. Bates is a graphics specialist at PricewaterhouseCoopers in the United States. Experienced in a wide range of graphics and design applications, Mr. Bates specializes in developing the graphical and multimedia components of new business proposals and presentations.

Peter Bittner, M.S., is a key member of the mySAP Workplace project team at SAP AG in Germany. In this position, he coordinates the development of industry-specific workplace roles. With a background in physics that includes practical experience in the design of integrated circuits, Mr. Bittner has co-authored several articles on the electrical characterization of semiconductors. These have appeared in a number of scientific journals. He is also experienced in the areas of product management and financial cost management, including activity-based costing.

Cory Coley, B. Comm., CA, is the director of strategic solutions at SAP in Canada. An IT professional with public accounting and financial management experience, Ms. Coley has spent 12 years working on ERP and other information technology implementations as both a corporate project and IT manager and as a consultant for SAP. In her current position, Ms. Coley helps SAP customers in a variety of industries to develop and implement winning e-business solutions.

Bernhard Drittler, Ph.D., is the project lead for the mySAP Workplace implementation at SAP AG in Germany. Dr. Drittler joined SAP as a software developer in the human resources application group. Subsequently, he was responsible for the development of SAP's Employee Self-Service and Human Resources Solutions.

David J. Duray, B.S., M.B.A., is a partner at PricewaterhouseCoopers and global leader of its SAP consulting practice—the largest practice of its kind. With more than 20 years of information technology experience, Mr. Duray has helped numerous Fortune 500 companies to implement and integrate SAP and e-business solutions. He is currently assisting SAP AG to develop mySAP Workplace industry role descriptions for 11 industries. A frequent speaker on technology topics, Mr. Duray's authoritative comments on SAP consulting matters can often be found in the business press and other major business media.

Juergen Heymann, Ph.D., is a member of the SAP AG organization, where he is senior architect of the mySAP Workplace. Based in Germany, Dr. Heymann has more than 10 years of information technology industry experience involving programming systems—both languages and environments—and Internet technologies. He is a frequent presenter and lecturer at SAP conferences.

James R. Hurley, B.A., M.B.A., CAGS, CPA, is a partner in PricewaterhouseCoopers' management consulting services practice and that organization's North American SAP practice leader for the telecommunications industry. Mr. Hurley specializes in e-business and ERP in the finance, telecommunications, and manufacturing industries. Co-author of *E-Business and ERP: Transforming the Enterprise* and *SAP: An Executive's Comprehensive Guide*, he has, for the past 15 years, worked at some of the world's largest consulting organizations, helping clients to apply technology to their businesses.

Bernd Kidler, B.S., is head of global field operations for marketing and lead generation at SAP AG in Germany. In that role, he initiates and drives key global initiatives aimed at improving the customer engagement model as SAP's go-to-market strategy. Mr. Kidler has more than 15 years of consulting experience in the information technology industry. His professional focus has been on change management and e-marketing.

Margret Klein-Magar, M.A., is a product manager at SAP AG in Germany. Currently focused on the mySAP Workplace, she has spent nearly a decade at SAP gaining expertise in knowledge management and playing a key role in other SAP initiatives, including EnjoySAP. A published author of several studies and articles on topics including electronic publishing and software ergonomics, Ms. Klein-Magar has lectured on information science at the University of Saarland.

Taya Leybman, B.A., works in PricewaterhouseCoopers' e-Learning group, where she focuses on knowledge management issues. Ms. Leybman's four years of project management, design, and implementation experience have involved her in projects ranging from custom-designed learning portals to SAP's knowledge management business scenario. Originally from Canada, Ms. Leybman is currently based in Germany at PricewaterhouseCoopers' European Centre of Expertise. She presently works on knowledge management delivery as it relates to the mySAP Workplace.

Brenda MacKay, B.A., works in the user integration group (UIG) at SAP Labs in the United States. In that role, she assists customers and software development groups to develop and implement software solutions that meet the needs of users. Ms. MacKay's more than 20 years of experience in the software industry includes positions as an applications developer, information architect, user integration specialist, and project manager. She has been a member of the SAP AG organization since 1990.

Claudia Mairon, M.B.A., is a member of the mySAP Workplace product management team at SAP AG in Germany and formerly a member of the product management team for Enjoy-SAP. In her current position, she works with customers to determine the product needs and requirements that form the basis of product planning and development. With a background in marketing and international management, Ms. Mairon has extensive experience in marketing research and statistical methods.

James Michael Nolen, B.A., is a principal consultant in PricewaterhouseCoopers' management consulting services practice. Based in the United States, he has consulted on the human dimensions, value proposition, and integration/collaboration issues related to enterprise portals. A professional with more than 12 years of experience in software development, integration, and implementation, Mr. Nolen has also consulted to major companies in the upstream oil and gas, transportation, and insurance industries, and worked with clients to help them better manage their information systems.

Grant Norris, B.S., M.B.A., is a partner in PricewaterhouseCoopers' management consulting services practice. Based in the United States, Mr. Norris has 17 years of experience designing and installing ERP and e-business systems for a variety of organizations in the telecommunications, transportation, defense, and energy industries. He has lectured on topics related to this experience at a number of software conferences and universities. Mr. Norris's global perspective results from his having lived and worked in Canada, Europe, the Middle East, and the United States. He is co-author of *E-Business and ERP: Transforming the Enterprise* and *SAP: An Executive's Comprehensive Guide.*

Jerry Quinn, B.S., M.B.A., is a principal consultant in PricewaterhouseCoopers' management consulting services practice. Based in the United States, he has 13 years of experience working with and consulting to a variety of telecommunications, chemical manufacturing, and financial services organizations. During the past four years, Mr. Quinn has helped major U.S.-based telecommunications companies implement successful ERP solutions. He currently assists companies in this market with their e-business initiatives. A frequent lecturer on technology and related topics, Mr. Quinn has delivered presentations on ERP technologies, business process reengineering (BPR), and e-business systems at major universities throughout the United States.

Prasanth K. Rasam, B.S., is a principal consultant in PricewaterhouseCoopers' management consulting services practice in the United States. An IT professional with over a decade of information processing experience, Mr. Rasam has been involved in consulting assignments covering all phases of custom system/application development and package implementation for clients in the insurance, telecommunications, manufacturing, finance, health care, information, entertainment, transportation, and high-tech industries. He is technically proficient in client-server, n-tier, and database technologies, and deeply experienced in CRM and package implementation. Mr. Rasam has published a number of articles on IT implementation issues.

Douglas E. Rogala, B.S., is a principal consultant in PricewaterhouseCoopers' management consulting services practice in the United States. His primary professional focus is on providing consulting services to clients in the financial services industry. Mr. Rogala has more than five years of project management experience helping companies to implement R/3 and mySAP.com products. Leveraging his financial services industry and SAP experience, he is currently working with SAP AG to develop insurance industry-specific role templates for the mySAP Workplace.

Carmen Ryan, B.M.S., CA, is a manager with PricewaterhouseCoopers' global risk management solutions practice. Having lived and worked in New Zealand, Ms. Ryan is now based in London, where she has focused on helping clients minimize IT systems risk. Currently, Ms. Ryan is involved in a number of major SAP implementations, including the mySAP Workplace.

Sven Schwerin-Wenzel, B.S., is a development manager at SAP AG in Germany. Since joining SAP in 1994, Mr. Schwerin-Wenzel has worked on numerous customer implementation projects, including many in the United States. In addition, he spent two years working as a senior developer in the R/3 simplification group in Palo Alto, California, and was responsible for the rollout of SAP's profile generator in the Americas. In his present position, Mr. Schwerin-Wenzel is responsible for overseeing the development of all role templates for the mySAP Workplace.

Michael Spaventa, B.A., is a communications specialist with the information development group at SAP Labs in the United States. In this role, he is responsible for managing various information design, training, usability testing, and multimedia development projects. A professional with more than 13 years of translation, documentation, and training experience, Mr. Spaventa has lectured at a number of national conferences on converting help environments to HTML.

Drew Strain, B.Sc., is a principal consultant in the management consulting services practice of PricewaterhouseCoopers in the United States. Mr. Strain's professional focus is on supply chain management. Having lived and worked in both Europe and the United States, he brings an international perspective to clients in the consumer packaged goods, chemical, and telecommunications industries. Over the past 10 years, he has helped companies in these industries to re-engineer processes and to implement ERP and e-business solutions. Mr. Strain is currently assisting SAP AG with the mySAP Workplace.

Ajay Tyagi, B.S., M.S., is a consultant in PricewaterhouseCoopers' management consulting services practice in the United States. Currently, he focuses on customer relationship management (CRM) solutions for companies in a variety of industries, including telecommunications, high tech, and pharmaceuticals. Mr. Tyagi also brings a rare blend of technical, functional, and marketing expertise to helping clients implement SAP, Siebel, and other e-business technologies. A professional with a global perspective, he has lived and worked in South Asia, the Middle East, and Europe.

Matthias Vering, M.S., is a Vice President at SAP AG in Germany and project leader for the mySAP Workplace. During his career at SAP, he has had extensive involvement in the R/3 and mySAP.com™ system development, including mySAP.com project and product planning and coordination of documentation and training. He has also led several cross-application projects, including certification of development and service in accordance with ISO9000 standards, and he was responsible for Enjoy-SAP, a precursor of the mySAP Workplace. Mr. Vering is the author of several publications on topics ranging from project management and information architecture to enterprise portals.

Gene Zasadinski, B.A., M.A., Ph.D., is a communications professional with more than 20 years of experience in both business and academia. Currently a director in the global thought leadership communications group at PricewaterhouseCoopers in the United States, he works with that organization's thought leaders to produce books, articles, white papers, presentations, and other major thought leadership vehicles focusing on cutting-edge business topics. Recent books for which Dr. Zasadinski has served as final editor include *Executive's Guide to E-Business: From Tactics to Strategy* and *E-Business and ERP: Transforming the Enterprise.*

Jon Zonderman, B.A., M.S., has over 20 years of experience writing for newspapers and magazines, authoring books, and teaching journalism and business writing. As a business-book ghostwriter, he has written over 25 books. Mr. Zonderman has been an editorial consultant on eight PricewaterhouseCoopers books, including *Executive's Guide to E-Business: From Tactics to Strategy,* and *ERP and E-Business: Transforming the Enterprise.* His work has appeared in national and regional publications, including *The New York Times Magazine* and *Technology Review.*

Index